LIGHT & UNSUPPORTED MOTORCYCLE TRAVEL FOR TERMINAL CASES

Being a treatise on touring by motorcycle in a practical and efficient manner.

• WIND • CAMPING • FOOD • GEAR • TIME & DISTANCE • PEOPLE • TRANSFORMATION •

Wind: Apparent and Ambient. Camping: Authorized and Unauthorized. Food: Stove or no Stove. Gear: Everyone will do this a little differently. Time and Distance: Daily Routines. People: Need them. Transformation: Why it feels good.

APPENDICES:

Cheap Equipment
Improvised Repairs
Camp Food Recipes
Navigation and Planning
Additional Reading
Useful Websites
The Usual Hangouts
Some Good Roads
All American Roads
Accommodations
Campgrounds
Gear Notes
Mileage Calculator
Measurement Conversions

Forward: What Is This?

This is a primer on lightweight touring. Which means riding a bike long distances in a manner familiar to our dusty predecessors. Meaning relatively simple equipment and just enough horsepower to get the job done. It means crossing state lines (maybe many) on far less than a liter's worth of propulsion. It means riding for the sake of riding--almost anything--without worrying about 'keeping up appearances' or having the latest and greatest. It means having a certain amount of grit, ingenuity, and self-reliance. It means doing things that some folks sneer at. It means going places they haven't. It means refining a personal system of travel based on hard experience. It means having a twinkle in your eye. It means being the Gasoline Stranger. It means being unexpectedly asked to tell tales at family functions, whether they approve of your pastimes or not. This is jarring the first time it happens, I assure you.

All the 'in front of the bar' posing in the world on a chrome-encrusted-what-have-you is a sad substitute for surveying a vista you've never seen. Or even fixing a decrepit bike in a rainy ditch with a strange ocean crashing its surf nearby. Or having to wait overnight for the only gas station to open because it closed at five.

I will always remember a letter to the editor of a motorcycle magazine many years ago. It was in reference to a sweepstakes drawing for whatever sportbike was in fashion at the minute. The writer stated that had he won the thing, he would have sold it in a second and used the proceeds to quit his job and tour the world on a Honda Trail 90. I don't know who he was, but he was a Wise Man. And I'll bet he's probably been more places and seen more things on two wheels than a lot of folks.

So if you're inclined or interested, give it a try. This little book was meant to help out. Heaven knows it's not for everybody. If you do get a taste for it and build up a store of experience and tales, you might run across another who's done similar. You'll both Get It, that's for sure. Enjoy.

LIGHTWEIGHT UNSUPPORTED MOTORCYCLE TRAVEL FOR TERMINAL CASES

Lightweight unsupported motorcycle travel means riding a forty to fifty horsepower, three to four hundred pound motorcycle, on a multi-day road trip, without a supply vehicle following behind. These machines typically ride best at under 75 mph, a speed slightly below the 80+ mph averages that are common on many limited access divided highways.

Motorcycles like this encourage a routing bias toward two-lane secondary roads. In addition to matching their speed capability better, secondary roads provide a more interesting mile-by-mile riding environment. Most two lane roads were built with different economic, social, and cultural considerations than those reflected in modern divided highways. The earlier the road, the nearer original roadside buildings will be to the shoulder, and the more closely the route will follow river courses and geographic contour lines.

This type of travel is inexpensive. Direct costs like gas (40-60 mpg), insurance ($150 - $300/yr), tires (+-$50 each), engine oil changes (2-3 liters per change), and the price of the motorcycle itself will all be less than the same expenses for larger bikes. Also, relocating a small motorcycle anywhere in the world via air cargo is less costly than shipping a larger, heavier one. Showing a lightweight motorcycle's license plate far away from home is fun. It makes you a Terminal Case.

• WIND • CAMPING • FOOD • GEAR • TIME &
DISTANCE • PEOPLE • TRANSFORMATION •

Wind:
Apparent and Ambient.

Few lightweight machines provide much wind protection. But having no windshield or body panels can be just fine. Average speeds are lower so shoulder and neck muscles can easily adjust to the apparent wind. It takes just a day or two. You will see much more without a windshield's layer of plastic to look around and through. And the wind's direct pressure helps keep average speeds lower so there's less chance of getting a ticket. Fighting head winds and enjoying tail winds also provides a sharper understanding of immediate meteorologic conditions. You'll better connect with the slightest changes in weather and front lines. Adjusting the throttle against varying ambient winds also provides a greater appreciation of the mechanical work that's being done to move everything along. It's an understanding that cannot be gained any other way. Finally, a helmet face shield unpredictably collects all kinds of bug splats. Each bigger hit sounds different, depending on the construction of the bug. Larger species with hard exoskeletons impact with a loud knock that's always a surprise.

Camping:
Authorized and Unauthorized.

Authorized camping means commercial campgrounds, state parks, national forests and other organized camping areas. There are no linked national reservation systems for campgrounds. Camping areas within a half-day's drive of major population centers are usually full on summer weekends. In general, the more remote the campground, the more available campsites it will have. *As I write this I'm at 6,200 ft elevation at the Deer Flat National Forest Campground which is on a 90 mile dirt road 'shortcut' between two state highways near Sun Valley, Idaho. Awesome scenery. Lots of firewood lying around. Clean pit toilets, a clear gurgling stream two feet away from my tent...and I'm the only camper here. In the last 12 hours just one vehicle has passed on this road. Plus, it's free. No $10.00 in an envelope in a steel slot canister. Free.* Asking for permission to camp on someone's property...like by a fire hall in a small town, or behind a church or private residence, is also a good way to find an overnight place. This is easier to arrange if you are alone or traveling with only one other rider.

Unauthorized camping means stealth campsites where nobody will see your camp. Good stealth spots can be around gravel pits, along power and pipe lines, behind hills, in acreage that's for sale, abandoned agricultural areas, ravines, forests, etc... places where landowners or caretakers are absentee or unlikely to be around in the short term. Well shaded, hidden areas with lots of underbrush are likely to have more bugs than open places. Look for access to seldom visited locations via overgrown or little used tracks and trails that lead away from the road and do not have mailboxes. Don't go past gates unless they're already open. Having a quiet muffler helps. So does making the camping decision about an hour to an hour and a half before twilight. Stealth campsite reconnaissance in the dark is all but impossible.

Food:
Stove or no Stove.

Without a camp stove you'll carry a food bag (anything from a large Aerostich envelope bag to a plastic grocery store bag) filled with canned or bagged tuna, sardines, canned beans, trail mix, fruit (dried and fresh), cookies, crackers, jerky, cheese, bread etc..., and will eat from this. Try using chopsticks to eat canned stuff like tuna and a classic, conventional spoon for campfire heated beans.

A small stove adds hot tea, potatoes, ramen noodles *(superb customized with fresh mushrooms, tomatoes, green peppers & canned salmon...mmm--add the salmon after cooking the rest, just before eating)*, and a variety of other wonderful things to the menu. Bring some salt, pepper and Tabasco sauce. Carry about 2-3 liters of water for daily camp drinking, cooking, brushing teeth, washing, etc.

Gear:
Everyone Will Do This A Little Differently.

Here's a setup for a trip of about 7,000 miles and 3 weeks that took place in August of 2001.

-**Bike** - 94 Honda XR650L, lowered motard conversion, bigger gas tank. *(see gear appendix A)*

-**Front Fender strap-on bag** - Aerostich electric vest (with on/off switch only-no thermostat) or a lightweight motorcycle cover. *(see gear appendix B)*

-**Number plate bag** - Located above the headlight, this is the bike's quickly removable 'tank bag'. Lip balm, cigarette lighter, Suunto computer instructions and spare battery, carbon fiber sidestand plate, microfiber face shield cleaning cloth, aspirin and ibuprofen, swiss army knife, sunglasses and reading glasses, spare earplugs in container, clearview shield sprayer, thermax glove liners, Aerostich Evap-o-Danna, sun hat, glove raincovers, Petzl Zipka LED flashlight. *(see gear appendix C)*

-**Handlebars** - Folding rear view mirror, Suunto Vector on custom mount (spare wristwatch + temp, time, alt, etc...), Cycoactive map case, Garmin GPS III, radar detector/radio bracket, Hi-lo electric grip switch. Flip-lever friction type cruise control. *(see gear appendix D)*

-**Aerostich Waterproof Side Zip Bag #1** - Tent, sandals, microfiber pants, long sleeve microfiber shirt, cell phone charger. Water bottle. Note: All (3) duffel and drybags are strapped on together under two Aerostich quick release straps. *(see gear appendix E)*

-**Aerostich Waterproof Side Zip Bag #2** - Thermarest 3/4 length pad, sleeping bag, Touratech LED tent light, bear spray. *(see gear appendix F)*

-**Aerostich Waterproof Side Zip Bag #3** - Microfiber towel, swimsuit, food bag, fleece sweater, daily trip journal in zippered cover. *(see gear appendix G)*

-**Ortlieb Small Drybag Duffel** - Two pairs fast drying wool/synthetic sox, Smartwool T shirt, two cotton T shirts, one pair blue jeans, two or three pairs underwear shorts (cotton, synthetic), cool weather gloves, Tank Bag Briefcase bag 'office' (with a couple of paperback books, money, receipt envelope, contact directory, road maps), stove, cook kit, food bag, folding water container, bathroom kit (Aero envelope bag with toothbrush, cup, soap, etc...), pocket am/fm/sw radio, camera and film. *(see gear appendix H)*

-**Rear fender tool bag** - Tools, bike owners manual, insurance and title, tire patch kit, Motion Pro multifunction tool, tire levers, co2 tire stuff, chain lube, prop stand, rag, inner tube strips, Cycoactive Tow Downs, C-H Bungee Buddy, spare ear plugs, inner tube (1). *(see gear appendix I)*

-**Darien Jacket** - Right sleeve pocket contains: Fingerlight LED flashlight, two Vee Wipe squeegees, spare earplugs. Logo pocket contains: cellular telephone. Inside pocket contains: cotton bandanna or paper towels. Left sleeve window pocket contains: ear plugs. *(see gear appendix J)*

-**Darien Pants** - Left front pocket contains: Wallet.
(see gear appendix K)

Time and Distance:
Daily Routines.

Firm deadlines and fixed destinations add pressures and complications to trips. A loose, flexible schedule is better. Trying to be done riding and off the road every day by five to seven pm will make most riding trips better. An average day can range between 150 and 500 miles, plus 100 miles if not camping out. Add another 100 if extended freeway riding is involved. When camping, a typical 400-450 mile two-lane-road day will start at 7-8 am. You'll be riding by 9-10 am and the day will end at an evening campsite around 7-8 pm. During the day, grocery, restaurant and scenic stops may total two or three hours. Six to ten hours will be spent in the ride-and-gas-stop mode. Making a lunch with a camp stove on a wayside table is a nice break. Achievable daily two-lane road distances will decrease east of the Mississippi and around populated areas and increase in the west and in remote areas.

People:
Need Them.

Motorcycle riding places one within a bubble of solitude that is both mesmerizing and deeply satisfying. Force yourself to break out of this state at regular intervals. Life is more than a scrolling tableau to be passively watched. Star Trek's famous 'Prime Directive' of non-interference is for outer space, not regular people in Kansas or Canada. One cannot have a good trip without interacting with some of the people encountered along the way. Make time to meet and know them. When engaging someone you won't have total control like you do over a motorcycle. But there are social skills and diplomatic techniques which help. Choose the times, places and ways to interact with locals that will catch people at their everyday best. Most people want to be helpful to you, and some will want to know about your life and trip.

Approaching those who do not ordinarily interact with large numbers of traveling strangers works best. The minimum wage cashier at a freeway interchange truck stop or c-store probably won't be as open as an individual raking their yard on a side street in a small town. Or a young rider sitting on a sport bike at the local roadside hangout. Inquire at fire halls or side street coffee shops about places to camp, not at busy interchange fast food restaurants. Traveling with a group of other riders makes it more difficult to engage locals but it's never impossible. Almost everyone watches TV and lives more private lives than was common a generation ago. It usually takes only a few moments to break through modern insularity and uncertainty and find commonalities. "What's cool around here? Good camping? Eating?" etc. Take off your helmet and riding gloves, run your hand through your hair and smile.

Transformation:
Why It Feels Good.

When you walk, bicycle, or motorcycle...and then camp, you participate in the world immediately around you in a unique way. These methods of living separate you from a house with its locks, windows and furniture. When you engage the world with only the intermediation of your clothing and the fabric of a tent, you learn stuff. You cannot lock a tent or perfectly shut out bad weather if you are living outdoors. Travel this way becomes a more transformational experience.

Car or camper trips are nice, but they are never as transformational as a motorcycle journey. Park a car anywhere and fall asleep. Inside you can lock out people and weather. You'll have windows, doors, shades, furniture, and most of the things you have at home. Most people are happy enough with windows, doors, and plumbing-at-the-ready lifestyles to want to have it with them wherever they go. I suppose they are not looking for deeper transformational experiences. At least not experiences that are as open ended and uncertain as living outdoors and on the road. Motorcycling and camping take advantage of the world's practically endless matrix of roads and infrastructure better than any other exposed, outdoor method of travel. Because it's so open and exposed, it's more profoundly transformational than regular 'capsulized' travel...which is why it always feels so good.

APPENDICES:

Cheap Equipment
Improvised Repairs
Camp Food Recipes
Navigation and Planning
Additional Reading
Useful Websites
The Usual Hangouts
Some Good Roads
All-American Roads
Accommodations
Campgrounds
Gear Notes
Mileage Calculator
Measurement Conversions

Not liable for errors or omissions. Send corrections or additions to <service@aerostich.com>

Cheap Equipment and Techniques

Waterproof packs are nice, of course, but think about how far you are going to be traveling in heavy rain for extended periods. How often has it happened? And what the heck is really wrong with those rather robust big zip-lock freezer bags they sell at the grocery store? Put your socks in one of those and keep 'em dry. Use garbage bags for larger items. A cheap drugstore flashlight with fresh batteries and a good bulb will get you through the darkest and longest night the same as a fancy model will. A simple folding pocket knife will hold an edge well enough to slice up an apple, spread peanut butter or open packaged snack foods. You are unlikely to ever need a 36" jungle machete or Navy Seals Combat Sheath Knife, even if you are riding to the Amazon via dangerous outlaw territories. You'll sleep warm and well inside any sleeping bag if you're tired from a long day of riding. The least expensive nylon and polyester sleeping bag will stuff compactly into small carrying bags for motorcycle traveling.

Some inexpensive gear and improvisational motorcycle travel techniques have been time tested and are well proven by generations of riders. A copy of the daily local newspaper purchased from a roadside store and wrapped around one's torso beneath a riding jacket really is a warm lifesaver on a cold ride. If they still have yesterdays edition, it will be free. Garbage bags worn inside boots but over socks help feet survive long cold rains. Dry and flattened corrugated cardboard boxes make very serviceable sleeping pads. Ask a homeless person. Any kind of surplus plastic sheeting makes a rainy campsite more comfortable. Wetting a T shirt costs nothing and makes riding through the hottest conditions a lot more bearable. Several ordinary shirts worn together are about as warm as one 'technical fleece' outdoor sweater. Some folded up tinfoil can almost function as a complete cook kit. Etc...

Preparation time and ingenuity are great equalizers. Purpose-built gear might be best, but this does not mean that perfectly serviceable moderate sized throw-over saddlebags cannot be made from army/navy surplus store gas mask pouches or inexpensive swap-meet salvage boxes or random garage sale finds. Cheap generic leather gloves from home and farm stores work fine for riding if they fit your hand well. The same goes for the simple dome tents and the other lightweight camping gear available at discount stores. Inexpensive fixed-length bungee cords can be custom-shortened to hold a load securely and neatly if you take the time to do this job.

Realistically anticipating moto-gear needs is simple. You probably won't need fancy stuff designed for every contingency. The lightest, most compact and stylish gear is ingenious and wonderful, but it's seldom a critical requirement. Like life insurance, most people tend to buy more gear-capability than they'll actually need. Just be safe and pay attention to what works and what doesn't. When you get back home, write down some equipment notes about what worked well and what didn't...while the bike is still warm, and before you forget anything you'd want to change next time. Finally, raingear made from garbage bags is terrible for anything except very short rides.

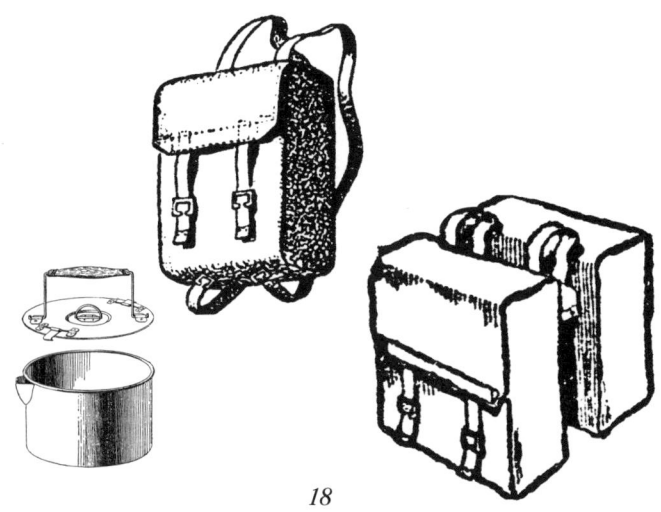

Improvised Repairs

Warning: Emergency repair procedures can involve hazards and risks to health, life and safety. Do not undertake improvised repairs or self-help procedures without first considering your own capabilities and circumstantial factors like weather, traffic conditions, etc... Your first responsibility is to safety.

Ask around any rally campfire about improvised 'get it home' emergency repairs and you'll hear some stories that are believable and others that aren't. All will be memorable. Like the one about the guy who rode ten miles across town holding the end of a broken throttle cable in his teeth while yanking down on the cable housing to gas the bike onward. (Ed at Aerostich has details.) This barely-a-repair improvisation actually got him home. A more common and classic tale involves clamping a locking pliers firmly onto the shift shaft after the gear lever fell or broke off. Many dirt bike riders have done this. How about the guy with the broken and dead battery who rode many miles to a rally following carefully close behind a friend's bike because his own bike's ignition system was functioning only via two ten foot lengths of wire stripped from non-essential parts of the wiring harness and strung from the healthy bike's battery to his bike's electrical system. Or how about the boat trailer tail light assembly that was hose clamped where the stock tail light was...after it went missing. Improvised repairs like these look terrible but can get you where you need to be.

General bodge principles:
A) Time matters - Don't rush any job, even if your riding 'friends' are screaming at you. Hurrying makes everything worse. Truly amazing field repairs are possible if you have enough time and patience.
B) Circumstances count - It's impossible to rebuild a leaking carb on the side of a busy freeway at midnight during a typhoon. Shut off the gas and push the pig elsewhere. Mechanical emergencies seldom occur at ideal locations or convenient times. If you must disassemble complex items directly over a grassy or earthen surface, first spread a cloth

beneath the work area. Use a shirt or a towel if you don't have a suitable rag. Even a wide flat board will do. Mother earth has a healthy appetite for tiny motorcycle parts.

C) React to the unusual - Half of the time it will turn out to be nothing but your mind playing paranoid tricks. But the rest of the time subtle changes will indicate actual problems. Is a strange vibration or new sound connected more with engine rpm's (?), or to the bumps and cracks on the road? If an unknown fluid suddenly appears on your boot or pant leg, pay attention to it. It won't go away by itself. And pay attention to routine stuff. Maybe the chain's masterlink clip really *has* fallen off.

D) Improvise - Many motorcycle parts are common enough to work across brands, applications and models. Non-interchangeable parts are sometimes surprisingly interchangeable. When disassembling things that are broken, never throw anything away, no matter how small. Everything fits somewhere. Even shards of bent, grenaded metal and fragged plastic may need to be pressed back into service with a little epoxy.

E) Electricity is magic - An artfully bent paper clip can replace a broken spark plug cap. Any piece of wire can jump a blown fuse, but make sure the short is corrected first. Carry a small multi-meter, some electrical tape and the bike's wiring diagram. Soldering can supposedly be done with a few match heads and a little piece of tinfoil if your name is MacGyver.

F) Helpful consumables - Duct tape, Miracle tape, JB weld, Super glue, etc. All are handy. Epoxy will patch a leaking steel gas tank. Position the leak above the gasoline level and go to it. Never, ever use silicone sealer around gasoline, like on a leaky petcock or anything. It will turn into a huge gelatinous napalm booger and cause problems.

G) Perseverance works - The motto "if at first you don't succeed, try, try again" is as true as always. Carefully disassembling anything that is not functioning and then putting it back together will solve or fix a hidden problem about 80% of the time. After you have tried this for the third time without success, take a break. Carefully lay every removed part out in sequential order so you can see how things go back together.

H) Cleanliness is good - Clean all disassembled parts fastidiously. Wipe, scrape, rub...use whatever is available and do whatever it takes. Then inspect each part completely. It is grand to motor off aboard a field-repaired machine even if you became grimy or made some clothing dirty in the process.

I) Know when to give up - Sometimes it is better to leave (hide?) the bike and seek help, or carry the dead machine away on a truck, or even occasionally tow it along behind another bike for a short distance. Gasoline and a lit match have never solved anything.

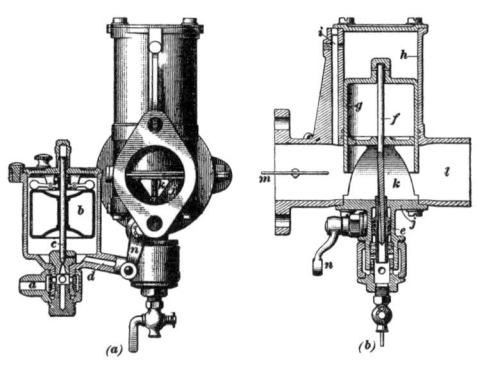

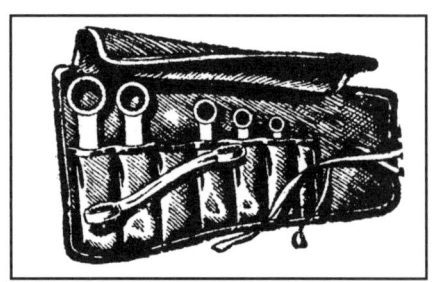

Camp Food Recipies

After a day in the saddle just about everything tastes good. On motorcycle trips, expensive freeze dried backpacking foods are not needed. There's plenty of perfectly trip-adaptable foods at the grocery stores along the way. The trick is to buy only a few items each day and refill your supplies at short intervals; One or two potatoes, a can of beans, a can of tuna, an onion, and a small loaf of bread are plenty if you re-provision every day or two. Doing this shopping takes only ten minutes, but is not as easy as it sounds. Try not to leave a giant market carrying a twelve pack and a sack of party snacks and junk food. Stay with the basics: Fresh bread, dry soups, noodles, canned items like tuna and beans, a couple of potatoes, one or two fresh veggies, etc. The items you select should resist spoiling in warm (or hot) storage for several days. For example, dark, bittersweet chocolate won't melt like all regular chocolates. And fresh meats won't keep as long as fruits and veggies. Have some jerky and a few energy bars as a nutritional backup. A typical day's menu might go something like this:

Breakfast: Fresh orange juice (bought the night before) plus bottled, flavored coffee or tea with a multigrain bar and an apple or other fresh fruit. Or several spoons of peanut butter and a banana. If you can generate hot water, try making instant oatmeal even though it's a little messy to clean up. Hot breakfasts are well worth the extra effort if you have the time and equipment. Single serving boxes of cold cereal are available at most c-stores. The denser varieties like 'Grape Nuts' and 'Granola' carry better. The 'breakfast of champions' of course, consists of eating a handful of instant coffee granules and lighting up a Lucky Strike straight. The breakfast of wimps is riding 50 miles then stopping at the best looking roadside restaurant and ordering an omelette and some pancakes.

Lunch: Beef jerky, instant hot soup, cheese and crackers, or deviled ham or peanut butter on bread or rye crackers. Sardines arranged in a neat row across a slice of fresh bread eat better than this sounds. Dark chocolate, 'Fig Newtons' or a sliced apple make an mmmm desert. A small can of 'V-8' or other fruit drink is good. Pre-made sandwiches in those triangular packs from c-stores are generally safe if they don't get too hot. Check the expiration dates, though. On hot days a small bag of salty chips will taste fantastic, but drink plenty of water, too. Whatever food is being promoted on the reader boards of roadside franchised restaurants will be your best caloric-buy, but the basic low-end menu items (like the cheapest plain burgers), are nutritionally safer. Less fat, etc. After lunch many people become slightly sleepy for a short period. A brief mid-afternoon nap on some shaded grassy area is safer than nodding off while riding.

Supper: If you are without a stove or a fire, or if it's already late and you are exhausted, then any cold food (like canned tuna on crackers) will do. But cooking something is always much better. Soup or a can of baked beans is so easy. So are ramen noodles, canned chili, stew, and other similar packaged items. Whole potatoes take a long time to bake, but if they are sliced up and combined with a few other veggies (mushrooms, green peppers, tomatoes) and wrapped inside a foil pouch, they will be ready in about ten minutes on a small campfire. Use low coals or a grate to minimize burning. Potatoes are delicious with only salt and pepper or with some barbecue or Tabasco sauce. Adding a few cut-up bits of fresh produce to packaged noodles or soups will make them enormously better. Roma or cherry tomatoes are less fragile and carry better than the larger beefsteak varieties. Cut up pieces of fresh mushrooms and onions add great flavors to most cooking projects. Purchase frozen meats and fish early in the day and they'll probably thaw just enough to be ready for cooking by evening. Keep frozen items in a plastic bag or somewhere condensation won't get other things wet. Corn on the cob is a good heat-and-eat grill food. It's also quite difficult to wreck grilled hot dogs. If you have a phone, sometimes near-urban camp spots are served by local delivery places. It's fun to order as you're pitching camp and take delivery just after everything is set up. If there is a restaurant near the last gas stop of the day, try buying a to-go dinner for later feasting - after you've found and made the camp. There's nothing like opening fresh hot pizza, a carton of shrimp fried rice, a package of fresh sushi, or a recently made deli sub sandwich...after the tent is up, the light is fading and you're ready to settle in. Bring along a flask of something or a few beers. Watch the stars. Read by flashlight. What the heck...

Navigation and Planning

Preliminary route planning is a good thing; but too much lessens the experiences of spontaneity, exploration and discovery. Some advance map reading - state highway maps, gazetteers, and mapping software - makes trips better, as does studying local guidebooks prior to starting out. But a detailed route picked at home may turn out all wrong when actually riding through the countryside. It is impossible to successfully make good decisions about where to go or which routes to take until you're actually out there. Better to use map study as an information source to locate items like river valleys, mountain ranges, and population centers (or lack of) -- things that influence traveling enjoyment. Don't overdo the research to the point that you've left little to discover along the way.

Some Nav/Plan Tips:
• Trip themes lead to interesting roads and places. Try Civil War battlefields, ferries, highest points or covered bridges. Almost anything can work for wandering the country 'on tour'.
• Full size gas station maps are bulky, but detailed maps are essential. Buy an oversize fifty state atlas and then tear it up, taking along only the pages needed. These oversize atlas maps contain nearly all the details of the larger folding maps.
•Downloadable GPS maps don't offer the planning and overview capability of a good printed map. 'Zooming out' eliminates the details needed to plan a day of good riding. A GPS plus a library of regular printed maps make the best combination.
• An old fashioned grease or wax pencil is more reliable than a felt tip highlighter. These can go dry unexpectedly and most types use an ink that will bleed if the paper gets wet. When tracing a route with a pen or pencil, do not trace directly over the road's line, but draw along parallel to it, about one eighth of an inch to the side. This leaves the original cartography intact. The 'double' line that results is more noticeable at a fast glance.

• Maps go out of date. Older maps show the cool early roads and places, but they also contain errors that can cause big navigational mistakes. Use any map over ten years old with caution.
• Magnetic compasses should be located as far away from ferrous metal as possible. Also, be aware that magnetic declination + deviation can be as much as 20º on some headings in some areas. Most good atlases have a small chart outlining the changes.
• Advance nightly lodging reservations are important during high seasons and conventions, and to insure accommodations at small resorts or bed and breakfasts.
• Unless you are trying for a surprise, give friends and relatives a few days notice. Arrive early enough to buy them dinner and so you can spend part of the evening together. Afterward, send a gift or thank you card.

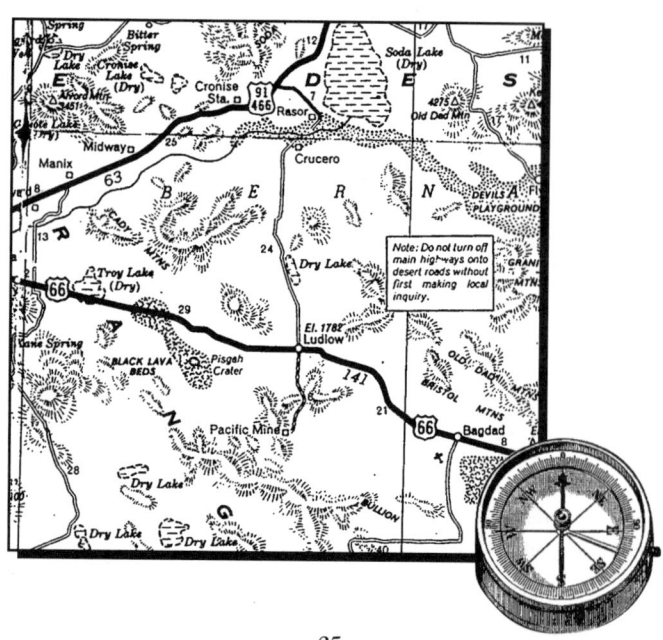

Additional Reading - Road Guides

Destination Highways: Washington
An astonishingly thorough rider's guide to riding in Washington state. By Brian Bosworth and Michael Sanders. 536 pp. ISBN: 0-9684328-1-6

Destination Highways British Columbia
A very comprehensive look at the riding situation in that part of the world. By Brian Bosworth and Michael Sanders. 475 pp. ISBN: 0-9684328-0-8

Motorcycle Journeys Through Northern Mexico
The author of this book has nearly thirty years' experience traveling in Mexico, and it certainly shows. By Neal Davis. 219 pp. ISBN: 1-884313-20-5

Baja Camping
While written for travelers of uh, the four-wheeled variety, this book offers valuable insight into traveling to this storied land of sun and surf. 230 pp. ISBN: 1-57354-069-2

Riding South
One needs to know about travel in the vast regions south of our border, all the way to Tierra Del Fuego, Machu Picchu, and Mexico's amazing Copper Canyon. By Dr. Gregory Frazier. 370 pp. ISBN: 0-935151-04-4

Europe By Motorcycle
This book is an essential guide for those entertaining a trip 'across the pond' to the old world. By Dr. Gregory W. Frazier. 280 pp. b/w illus. ISBN: 0-935151-49-4

Motorcycle Journeys Alps
This book covers every region of the Alps with an attention to detail that will make your trip there fantastic. By John Hermann 223 pp. ISBN: 1-884313-12-4

Alaska by Motorcycle
A trip to the United States wildest corner and how to do it. Based on extensive experience. By Dr. Gregory W. Frazier. 190 pp. ISBN: 0-935151-47-8

The World Famous Alaska Highway
This book is a great way to familiarize the would-be traveler with the conditions and opportunities that are on and along this storied stretch of road. By Tricia Brown. 288 pp. ISBN: 1-55591-446-2

Arkansas Rider's Guide
A book for motorcycle junkies who see destinations as an excuse to carve corners on twisting, forested mountain roads and find beautiful, unexpected scenery in out-of-the-way places. By Mario Caruso. 144 pp. ISBN: 0-9718973-0-1

Motorcycle Journeys Through Baja
Based on 20 years of experience traveling the lesser-known byways of the Baja Peninsula. By Clement Salvadori. 240 pp. ISBN: 1-884313-08-6

Motorcycle Journeys Through California
This guidebook will have you riding prime roads and seeing beautiful and interesting sights all over the Golden State. By Clement Salvadori. 319 pp. ISBN: 1-884313-18-3

Road Trip USA California And The Southwest
Myth, beauty, and actual history of the west that makes for fascinating travel and spectacular vistas. By Jamie Jensen. 482 pp. ISBN: 1-56691-190-7

Motorcycle Journeys Southwest
This book describes 66 separate rides, each about a day in length and each including great roads and awesome scenery. By Marty Berke. 360 pp. ISBN: 0-9621834-9-0

Driving the Pacific Coast: Oregon and Washington
The picturesque northern reaches of the northwest are yours to explore with this comprehensive guide to the scenic coastal highways and roads of this area. By Kenn Oberrecht. 241pp. ISBN: 0-7627-0137-4

Driving the Pacific Coast: California
If you've ever wanted to cruise the scenic coast of California, and want a savvy guide to let you know just where all the best spots for inns, beaches, vineyards and local happenings, this is for you. By Kenn Oberrecht. 241 pp. ISBN: 0-7627-0713-5

Motorcycle Journeys Appalachians
Besides great scenic mountain roads and backwoods towns isolated in narrow valleys you will also learn about the history and diversity of this amazing part of the world. By Dale Coyner. 319 pp. ISBN: 1-884313-02-7

Motorcycle Journeys New England
A terrific guide and trip planner that includes 19 plotted routes of exceptional interest. By Marty Berke. 224pp. ISBN: 0-9621834-8-2

Great American Motorcycle Tours
Contains 20 localized backroad tours. By Gary McKechnie. 362 pp. ISBN: 1-56261-440-1

Scenic Driving Back Country Byways
Explore the vast spaces of America's west with this guide to forty-five outstanding scenic drives located in eleven states. By Stewart M. Green. 277 pp. ISBN: 1-56044-951-9

The New Roadside America
If you are looking for the unusual to spice up a roadtrip, this is a good source of some seriously offbeat info on America's oddest tourist attractions. By Mike Wilkins, Ken Smith, and Doug Kirby. 287 pp. ISBN: 0-671-76931-6

Road Trip USA America's Two-Lane Highways
Spanning the United States are a network of roads that have been largely supplanted by more modern, bigger, and infinitely duller interstate highways. This book is about exploring these backroads and their hidden treasures. By Jamie Jensen. 784 pp. ISBN: 1-56691-396-9

Additional Reading - General Information

The Complete Idiot's Guide To Motorcycles
A great up-to-date 'ground zero' guide to motorcycling for the novice or beginning rider. Written in a friendly, explanatory prose, this book takes the neophyte through the kinds of bikes and riders that are out there, as well as what would make a good beginner machine (plus what to look for when you buy). Other sections include the topics of street survival, maintenance, and the motorcycling community. By the editors of *Motorcyclist Magazine*, with Darwin Holstrom. 395 pp. ISBN: 0-02-862416-5

Motorcycle Owner's Manual
Not a brand-specific manual but very concise and informative. A good book for those with questions on bike maintenance and mechanics. Ideal for new riders or those who want to get involved in their bikes' maintenance. Richly endowed with illustrations and diagrams, this well-produced book is a great way into the brotherhood of the greasy hand. By Hugo Wilson. 112 pp. ISBN: 0-7894-1615-8

Bike Log
A decidedly low-tech but effective way of keeping track of what it is you put into and on your motorcycle in the way of upkeep and maintenance. Included are pages for service logs, trip data, oil changes, and many other things: storage checklist, bike specs, English/Metric conversion etc. Small enough to fit in a jacket pocket. 3.6" x 5.5".

Motorcycle Touring
A definitive "how to" for traveling long distances by motorcycle. Written with an intimate storyteller's style, this comprehensive compendium is fun reading that will leave your head full of stuff you'll remember when needed. Of particular interest are the many stories about how to deal with things that go wrong, and how to prevent things from going wrong. Entertaining as hell. By Greg Frazier. 160 pp. Softbound. 8.25" x 10".
ISBN:0-7603-2035-7

Camping's Top Secrets
Detailed and concise writing coupled with a dash of humor results in a very readable and informative book that is packed with hundreds of tips on living outdoors and dealing with the vagaries of mother nature as well as those of camping equipment. All sorts of other insights on staying dry, warm (or cool), coping with insects and minor injuries, eating, drinking, sheltering, and just about anything else that can come up when you're in the great outdoors. By Cliff Jacobson. 288 pp. ISBN: 0-7627-0391-1

Motorcycle Camping Made Easy
A no-nonsense primer on heading out on the scoot to camp. Valuable tips and practical techniques relayed here will point you in the right direction if you are interested in going to bike rally events or perhaps heading out on your own for a bit of remote solitude. Real-life issues like assessing a bike for load-carrying ability. Camp skill basics like starting a fire and cooking are covered as well as info on finding motorcycle-friendly campsites, along with all the rest you'll want to know. By Bob Woofter. 128 pp., ISBN: 1-884313-33-7

Free Campgrounds East/West
These books cover the surprising amount of no-cost camping available across our country, maybe even near where you live or are planning to travel. Thousands of locations are listed by state and city, with detailed directions to each campground and information about facilities and activities available at each one. Find little-known and free campgrounds. By Don Wright. East 450 pp., ISBN: 0-937877-40-9 West 480 pp. ISBN: 0-937877-41-7

Useful Websites

USA-Events and Attractions

Area Guides	www.areaguides.net
Festivals	www.festivals.com
Find A Grave	www.findagrave.com
Hidden America	www.hiddenamerica.com
Infiltration (abandoned bldgs)	www.infiltration.org
Largest Roadside Attractions	www.wlra.us/
Let's Ride	www.lets-ride.com/ridesevents.htm
MN's Roadside Architecture	www.mnhs.org/places/other/roadside
MuseumSpot.com	www.museumspot.com
Roadside America	www.roadsideamerica.com
Roadside Art 1	http://interestingideas.com/roadside/roadside.htm
Roadside Art 2	www.savvycenter.com/explorer/roadside/roadside.htm
Roadside Art 3	http://www.roadsidepeek.com/roadside/roadart/
Roadside Diner Guide	www.dinercity.com
Soc. for Commercial Archeology	www.sca-roadside.org

USA-Roads and Routing

California Motorcycle Roads	www.pashnit.com/motoroads.htm
CA Realtime Freeway Map	www.dot.ca.gov/traffic
Freetrip Roadtrip Routing	www.freetrip.com
Geocode - Address Routing	www.geocode.com/modules.
GPS Waypoint Registry	www.waypoint.org
Interstate Wizard	www.interstatewizard.com
Los Angeles Area Traffic:	www.traffic.com/LA-East/East-LA-Traffic-Reports.html
Most Dangerous Intersections	www.statefarm.com/di/danpress.htm
National Traffic Info	www.fhwa.dot.gov/trafficinfo
NSBO - Scenic Byways	www.byways.org/index.html
Parking Pal	www.parkingpal.com
Places2ride.com	www.places2ride.com

Plan Your Roadtrip	www.exitsource.com
Ridin' Roads	hea-www.harvard.edu/motorcyclist/roads.html
River Roads	www.riverroads.com
Road Condition Report	www.beaverbear.com/hwycond.html
Road Construction	www.randmcnally.com/rmc/tools/roadConstructionSearch.jsp
RoadTrip America	www.roadtripamerica.com
Route 40	www.route40.net/index.shtml
ROUTE 66	route66.netvision.be
ROUTE66	www.historic66.com/
Route 66 Federation:	www.national66.com/
Scenic Byways	www.byways.org
Southwest	www.swbike.com
Sport Bike Roads	www.execpc.com/~ytk/frconten.htm
Superior Byways	www.superiorbyways.com
The Great Divide Tour	www.whizmoandgizmo.com/DivideTour02
The Great RAT Run (2000):	http://ourworld.compuserve.com/homepages/DavidEBSmith/cycle/rat2000/RAT2000.htm
The Great RAT Run (1999):	http://ourworld.compuserve.com/homepages/DavidEBSmith/cycle/rat1999/rat99.htm
The Lincoln Highway	www.lincolnhighwayassoc.org
Top Motorcycling Roads	62west.net/bikers/roads.html
Traffic Congestion	www.fhwa.dot.gov/congestion
Traffic Doc	www.trafficdoc.com
Traffic Reports	www.traffic.com
Trans America Trail	www.transamtrail.com/main.htm
TRIP: Road Information	www.tripnet.com

USA-Accommodations

Bed and Breakfast Inns	www.bbonline.com
Camp/Campground Reservations	www.reserveamerica.com
Cheapest Deals	www.cheapestdeals.com
Free Campgrounds	www.freecampgrounds.com
Hostels.com	www.hostels.com
Homestays	www.servas.org

Quik Book	www.quikbook.com
Room Saver	www.roomsaver.com
The Savvy Traveler Web Site	www.savvytraveler.com
Wacky Hospitality Sites	www.unlv.edu/Tourism/wacky.html

USA-Miscellaneous

American Autobahn	www.americanautobahn.com/
Gas Price Watch	www.gaspricewatch.com
Hurt 911, Injury Info	www.hurt911.org
Jam Lasers	www.motorists.com/MI/laser.html
Photo Cop	www.photocop.com
Police Speed Measuring System	www.copradar.com
Radar Jammers	www.jamradar.com
Radar Test	www.radartest.com
Reasonable Drivers Unanimous	www.ibiblio.org/rdu
Riding on Public Land	www.recreation.gov
Speed Trap Exchange	www.speedtrap.org
Speeding Tickets	www.speedingticket.net
Speed Traps	www.streetracing.org/speedtraps/
The Ticket Assassin	www.ticketassassin.com
Traffic Radar Handbook	www.copradar.com/preview/content.html
Traffic Ticket Info	www.traffic-ticket.com
Ultimate Police Car Photos	www.geocities.com/MotorCity/Downs/2941

International Riding

10 Years on 2 Wheels	www.globeriders.com
Adventure Traveling	www.comebackalive.com
Air Medivac Service	www.internationalsos.com
All Hotels	www.all-hotels.com/home.htm
Cheap Nights	www.cheapnights.com
Cyber Cafe's	www.cybercafes.com
European MC Travel Tips	www.munnwerks.combmw/eurotips.html
Expat Tips	www.expatexchange.com
Global Freeloaders	www.globalfreeloaders.com
Global Internet Cafe's	www.netcafeguide.com

Global ISP Roaming (GoRemote)	www.goremote.com
Global Volunteers	www.globalvolunteers.org
Horizons Unlimited	www.horizonsunlimited.com
Inn Site	www.innsite.com
International Motorcyclers	www.rio.com/~tynda
Intermot Show	www.intermot-muenchen.de/
Intl. Motorcycle Shipping	www.micapeak.com/~marcl/pages/shipbike.html
Intl. Travel Insurance	www.worldtravelcenter.com/eng/index.cfm
Intl. Shipping #1	www.motoship.com
Intl. Shipping #2	www.motorcycleexpress.com
Intl. Shipping #3	www.gate.net/~bikeship
Internet Access - Global	www.atlas.co.uk
Isle Of Man TT	www.iomtt.com/
Lonely Planet	www.lonelyplanet.com
Med Assist/Jet Evac Worldwide	www.ijet.com
Travel Ins&Med Assist Intl Travel	www.medexassist.com/index.html
UK Gov International Travel Info	www.fco.gov.uk/travel
UK Places	www.geocities.com/MotorCity Garage/8738/bikemeet.html
UK Roads 2	www.bytefactory.com/mcycleindex.shtml
UK Speedtraps	www.ukspeedtraps.co.uk/
US State Dept. Int'l Travel Info	travel.state.gov/travel/warnings.html
World Time Server	www.worldtimeserver.com
Worldwide Travel and Medical Ins	www.internationalpro.com

Mexico Riding

Baja Expo	www.bajaexpo.com
Baja Links	www.bajalinks.com
Baja Weather Service	www.baja-cabo.com/weather.html
Baja.org	www.baja.org
Discover Baja	www.discoverbaja.com
Driving Info	www.mexonline.com/drivemex.htm
Online Baja Links	www.mexonline.com/baja/links.htm

GPS's

Garmin	www.garmin.com
General GPS info	www.joe.mehaffey.com
GPS w/your Mac	www.gpsy.com
GPS Waypoint DataBank	www.swopnet.com/waypoints
GPS Waypoint Reg	www.waypoint.org
Waypoint Base	www.waypoints.de

Moto-Guides and Forums

Adventure Rider Forums	www.advrider.com/forums
BBC-How to Ride a MC	www.bbc.co.uk/h2g2/guide/A271720
Bike Safety	www.motorcycle.com/mo/mcnews/safety.html
Dirt Rider Net	www.dirtrider.net
Maintenance	bongo.www8.50megs.com/maintenance.htm
Mark Ketchum's MC Page	www.ketchum.org/moto.html
Short Biker List FAQ	www.nebcom.com/noemi/motosbl.faq.html
Traveling with a Laptop	www.roadnews.com
Woods Racers	www.woodsracer.com

4-sale

2WheelSales.com	www.2wheelsales.com
CycleSales Classifieds	www.cyclesales.com
Harley Classifieds	skyway99.com/American-Motorcycle-Photoads/harleys-4sale.htm
Motor bike checklist	www.zip.com.au/~cs/moto/FAQs Used_Bike_Checklist.html
Motorcycle Leather Exchange	members.aol.com/motorle/index.html
Motorcycle Reports	www.mcreports.com
Motorcycle Online Classifieds	www.motorcycle.com/mo/classified
Salvage yards	www.moto-directory.com/salvage.asp
Salvage Yards 2	www.cyclemallusa.com/salvage/index.html
Used Bike Evaluation Guide	www.clarity.net/~adam/buying-bike.html
Used bike value guide	www.mcnews.com/mcnews/articles/ubvg99.html

Motorcycle Manufacturers

BMW	www.bmwmotorcycles.com/home
Buell	www.buell.com
Ducati	www.ducatiusa.com
Harley Davidson	www.harley-davidson.com
Honda	www.hondamotorcycle.com
Kawasaki	www.kawasaki.com
KTM	www.ktm.co.at
Moto Guzzi	www.motoguzzi-us.com
MZ	www.motorradna.com
Norton	www.nortonmotorcycles.com
Rokon	www.rokon.com
Spagthorpe	www.spagthorpe.com
Suzuki	www.suzuki.com
Triumph	www.triumph.co.uk
Victory	www.victory-usa.com
Ural	www.ural.com
Yamaha	www.yamahausa.com

Maps

British Ordnance Survey Maps	www.ordsvy.gov.uk
Canadian Topographic Maps	maps.NRCan.gc.ca
Expediamaps	www.expediamaps.com
Geodetic Survey of Canada	www.geod.nrcan.gc.ca
How far is it?	www.indo.com/distance
Mapblast	www.mapblast.com
MapQuest	www.mapquest.com
Maps on us	www.mapsonus.com
More Maps	www.freetrip.com
Motorcycle Roads US	www.motorcycleroads.us
National Atlas of Canada Online	www.atlas.gc.ca
Topographic Maps	www.topozone.com
Eagle Geocoder	www.geocode.com/eagle.html-ssi

Weather

Center for Atmospheric Research	www.ncar.ucar.edu/ncar/index.html
Intellicast	www.intellicast.com
Live Weather Images	www.weatherimages.org
Monthly Moon Phases	home.hiwaay.net/~krcool/Astro/moon
Old Farmers Almanac	www.almanac.com
Pilot Weather Briefing	www.pilotweatherbriefing.com
Pole to Pole Weather	www.poletopole.org
The Heat Index	www.nsis.org/weather/heatindex.html
The Weather Channel	www.weather.com
TruckerWeather.com	www.truckerweather.com
Weather Information Network	weather.gov

Directories & Indexes

Bikelinks - MC Site List	www.dropbears.com/bikelinks/index.htm
Rider's Rights	ridersrights.org International
Micapeak	www.micapeak.com
MC Distance Pieces and Parts	home.earthlink.net/~webmaster10/ld
Moto directory	www.moto-directory.com
Normal Motorcycling Links	www.bikergirl.net/links.html
Ronnie Cramers Index	sepnet.com/cycle/index.htm

Associations

AHRMA	www.ahrma.org
AMA	www.ama-cycle.org
American Hwy Users Alliance	www.highways.com
Bald Guys Motorcycle Club	www.baldguysmc.com/
Blind Lizards Motorcycle Club	www.blindlizards.com/
FIM	www.fim.ch/en/default.asp
Denizens of Doom	www.denizensofdoom.org
Denizens of Doom FAQ	www.denizensofdoom.com
FSSNOC	www.perardua.net/FSSNOC/FSSNOC.HTML
IBMC	www.ibmc.org
Iron Butt	www.ironbutt.com
Motorcycle Riders Foundation	www.mrf.org

Motorcyclist Rights Orgs	weaselsusa.org/mro.htm
National Motorist Association	www.motorists.org
Ride To Work	www.ridetowork.org
RideHSTA	www.ridehsta.com
Women On Wheels	www.WomenOnWheels.org

Moto Culture

American Angst	www.goingfaster.com/angst/main.htm
BADD-Bikers Against Drunk Drivers	www.baddcentral.com
Bad MC's for Bad People	www.stormloader.com/users/manzruin/index2.html
Beer Keg Rack	www.infernalmachineshop.com/Keg_Rack_1.htm
Biker Bob's Harley Site	www.angelfire.com/on/BikerBob/enter.html
Blackfly 1600	www3.sympatico.ca/peterhh/blackfly1600.htm
Bubba Zanetti	www.geocities.com/irishdaffy/
CB 750 Mutilation Society	www.cb750choppers.com
Dogs On Bikes	www.dogsonbikes.com/
Fred Gassit Bikerama	members.tripod.com/fredgassit
House of Cool Beemers	motorrad.cx/cool
Ice Road Racing	www.iceroadracing.net/
Lugeless Pavement Racers	www.malehorn.com/Lugelessness/Default.htm
MCMovieDatabase	http://motorbiker.org/Motorbiker.nsf/Movies_Welcome?OpenForm
MC Paper Craft	http://freepapertoys.com/pt-motorcycle.html
MC Paper Craft - Yamaha	21yamaha.com/mc/papercraft
Mental Scenery	www.bikergirl.net/trips/index.html
Michelle Duff	www.michelleduff.ca
Motorcycle Explorer	www.motorcycleexplorer.com
Motorcycho	ratbike.org/motorcycho/mchopage.html
NYC-Moto Home Page	www.magpie.com/nycmoto
Peraves Eco Mobile	www.peraves.ch/ndexe.htm
Phantom Oiler	www.vintagenet.com/phantom
Rev Sinclair MC Hearse	www.fasterpastor.com
Robot Motorcycle	www.ghostriderrobot.com/
Russian Motorcycles	www.kamaz.ru/motorcycles/index.htm
San Fransisco MC/Scooter Coalition	www.sfmsc.org

Sickest Bikes	http://sickestbikes.dyndns.org/home.htm
Sport Rides Streaming Video	www.roadmc.com/default.asp
Squidlys.com	www.squidlys.com
Sturgis Main Street WebCam	www.damnbikers.com/images/sturgiswebcam.htm
The 751	the751.tri-pixel.com
Track Junkie	www.trackjunkie.com/index2.htm
Trial Riding Game	www.dnainternet.fi/pelit/english
Will England's Notes	http://will.mylanders.com/outdoors/motorcycle/notes/

Misc. Entertainment

Bartleby.com: Great Books Online	www.bartleby.com
BlastHaus	www.blasthaus.com
Britannica.com	www.britannica.com
Green Highway	www.greenhighway.net
Halfbakery	www.halfbakery.com
How Do You Drive?	www://windward.nodalpoint.net/doc/media/liikenne.swf
JunkScience	www.junkscience.com
Magic 8-ball	ofb.net/8ball/procedure.html
Problems of the Future	www.newgrounds.com/
Online Originals	www.onlineoriginals.com
QuackWatch	www.quackwatch.com
Radar Jammers and Detectors	integrity.eburg.com
Rubic's Java Applet	http://www.schubart.net/rc/
Space Age Racing	www.tecaeromex.com/ingles/sar-i/index.html
Survival Research Laboratories	www.srl.org
Suite101	www.suite101.com
The Internet Public Library	www.ipl.org
TheSmokingGun	www.thesmokinggun.com
Torq Grip	www.sheldonbrown.com/tork-grip.html
Ultimate Poseur's SUV Page	poseur.4x4.org

Magazines/Webzines

2 Wheeled Freaks	www.2wf.com
Bike UK	www.motorcycleworld.co.uk
Canadian Biker	www.canadianbiker.com
CybercycleMag	www.cybercyclemag.com
Cyclenews	www.cyclenews.com
Cycle World	www.cycleworld.com
MN MC Monthly	www.motorbyte.com
MotoDirectory	www.moto-directory.com
Motorbiker Blog	http://blogs.motorbiker.org/mikewerner/Blog.nsf/
Motorcycle Consumer News	www.mcnews.com
Motorcycle Daily	www.motorcycledaily.com
Motorcycle News	www.motorcyclenews.com
Motorcycle Newswire	www.motorcyclenewswire.com/news.cfm
Motorcycle Online	www.motorcycle.com
Motorcyclist	www.motorcyclistonline.com
Motoworld	www.motoworld.com
Performance Bike UK	www.motorcycleworld.co.uk
Ride A Motorcycle Webzine	www.rideamotorcycle.com
Rider	www.ridermagazine.com
RoadracingWorld	www.roadracingworld.com
Scooters and Girls	www.scootergal.com/
Track Junkie	www.trackjunkie.com/index2.htm
Trail Rider	www.trailrider.com
Twistgrip	www.twistgrip.com
WomanMotorist	www.womanmotorist.com/index.php/welcome

The Usual Hangouts

Cafe Veloce (**Seattle, WA**) Italian restaurant with all kinds of bikes. Weekend evenings. Locals, Lazy B mechs, and destination diners. I-405 N to 12514 120th Ave NE, Kirkland WA. 425-814-2972

Alki Tavern (**Seattle, WA**) Taco Thursday. 1321 Harbor Ave. SW, Seattle, WA 98116. Come into Seattle on 90 going west. Go left (south) on 99, go right (west) on West Seattle Bridge. Go right (north) on Harbor Ave. Drive. Go past California Way SW, but don't turn on it. Ride a little ways, you're there. 206-932 9970.

8th Street Sports Bar & Grill (**Seattle, WA**) Sportbike Night. 10833 8th St. NE, Bellevue, WA 98004. 425-452 5617. They open at 4:00 p.m. Call for directions.

Planet Georgetown (**Seattle, WA**) The 500 member Vintage Motorcycle Enthusiasts meet the first Wednesday of each month. Brit stuff, moderns, and a great club. 6266 13th Ave. So. Seattle, WA 98108 206-762-4009. I5 to S. Albro Place West, right on 13th Ave. South.

Max's Tavern (**Eugene, OR**) Bar and grille. All kinds of bikes, esp on 'Motorcycle Monday', which falls naturally on every Monday. Hip. Located at 550 E. 13th Ave., Eugene, OR. 541-485-9001. From 105, take exit (South) to #99 Coburg Rd. Go left (west) to East Broadway. Go South (right) on Patterson St. Go right on 13th Avenue.

Fox 'n Firkin (**Corvalis, OR**) Bar/pub with authentic britpub food. Friday afternoons and evenings. Mostly HD but always a nice mix of euro scoots. 2002 SW First St. Corvallis, OR 541-753-8533. Take Corvallis/Lebanon exit on I-5. Go 20 miles to First Street in Corvallis (by the river). Can't miss it.

The Wall (**San Francisco, CA**) Scenic overlook turn out. Sportbikes, hardcore commuters. Daily, late afternoons until just after sunset. I-80 to

580 to US Hwy 24 north to Fish Ranch Rd, exit North to Grizzly Peak Blvd (rt), turnout is 3 miles on bay side. Only overlook with actual wall you can sit on.

Zeitgeist (**San Francisco, CA**) Friday night & Sunday afternoons are best (and most weeknights). Urban bike bar with bicycle & motorcycle couriers. 199 Valencia (at Duboce St.) Hwy 101N to Mission St. Exit, straight 2 blocks on right side. Across From Scuderia West shop. 415-255-7505.

Alice's Restaurant (**San Francisco, CA**) Sunday mornings. All kinds of bikes and bikers. Scott Flying Squirrels to AMF Harley mopeds. Roadside restaurant. 101 to Hwy 84 west 4 miles to Hwy 35 and you're there (at this crossroad). Also check out 'The Merry Prankster' restaurant another 8 miles west down 84. It's across from 'Applejacks' a popular H-D hangout where they do a good Sunday afternoon bbq.

Rock Store (**Los Angeles, CA**) Convenience store and outdoor cafe. Exit West off 101(Kanan Rd.), go South, left on Troutdale Rd. Right on Mulholland Highway. Saturdays and Sundays. World's best poseurs on every kind of bike plus assorted real regulars and everyday hardcore riders.

Newcombs Ranch (**Los Angeles, CA**) Restaurant-ski chalet. Exit the 210 Freeway west of Pasadena at Angels Crest Highway exit. Sunday around lunchtime. Mostly sportbikes. Go on to the tunnels and get someone with a Duck to ride through fast. Take your helmet off and enjoy God's own reverb.

Cooks Corner (**Los Angeles, CA**) Roadhouse restaurant & bar. Saturdays and Sundays. 7 am-9 pm. Breakfast, lunch, dinner. I-5 to El Toro Rd, go east 6-7 mi to Cooks Corner. Lots of Hardly Ableson's in the sunshine and also the occasional sportsy bike collection.

Lookout Roadhouse (**Los Angeles, CA**) Restaurant, bar and B&B. 8 am-7 pm everyday, Saturday and Sunday mornings. Sportbikes, sportbiques, n'sportsyheads. I-5 or I-15 to Cal 74, 32107 Ortega Hwy, Lake Elsinore, CA. 909-678-9010 Ask for Barbara (owner).

Village Coffee Roaster (**Los Angeles, CA.**) Every Wednesday at 8pm, ride leaves to eat somewhere. 101 freeway exit Mulholland/Valley Circle, left (south) over freeway on Valley Circle. Located in shopping plaza on left by Bank of America. 23351 Mulholland Dr., Woodland Hills, CA 818-591-2366

McGee's Grill (**Citrus Heights, CA,** a suburb of Sacramento) 5623 Sunrise Blvd. See website on www.sportbikenight.com for the next event. Promoter: Mike Summer. Dudes, mainly. Directions on website.

Sagebrush Cantina (**Calabasas, CA**) Bar and Grill. Los Angeles Quiche Bike Couture Culture. Sunday Afternoons. Sportbikes, euro's and Kustom Harley. Kase of the Kools. Mullholland exit off the 101 freeway. 22527 Calabasas Road, Calabasas, CA 818-222-6062

Wolf's Grill (**Pine Mtn, CA**) Restaurant at the Pine Mtn Inn. Sunday. Sport bikes in the AM and cruisers in the afternoon. Britbikes and Eurobikes at irregular intervals. 30 miles N of Ojai, CA on delicious Hwy 33. The middle of Nowhere.

Live Wire (**San Diego, CA**) Restaurant/Bar. Tuesdays, late evenings. Euro and sport riders. 2103 El Cajon Blvd. 619-291-7450. Corner of El Cajon and Alabama St.

PJ's & Co. (**Reno, NV**) Saloon and restaurant menu. Every Wednesday night year around, with only a few in the winter, but over a hundred in the summer. All kinds of cool rides, with some fast'n sporty ones...it's Nevada, duh. 1590 S. Wells Ave. 775-323-6366. Directions: Take I-80 to South Wells Ave. Located on the left.

ACME Bar & Grill (**Phoenix, AZ.**) Weekend bike nights. All kinds of bikes and bikers. Zoot deco artsy with a bike hanging above the bar. Pool tables, weekly events and live performances. 4245 N. Craftsman Ct. 407-644-6636. Directions: Take AZ-143N to East McDowell Rd., left on N 64th St., right on East Indian School Rd., right on N. Goldwater Blvd., right on E 3rd Ave., left on N. Craftsman Ct.

Billet Bar (**Phoenix, AZ.**) Mostly upscale Harley riders. Sushi, appetizers, omlettes, subs, pizzas, burgers. Pool tables. 3752 N. Scottsdale Rd. 480-941-1876. Directions: Take AZ-143 N to East McDowell Rd., left on N 64th St., right on East Indian School Rd., left on Scottsdale Rd. Located on the left.

Dulonos Pizza (**Minneapolis, MN**) Pizza restaurant. First Thursday of the month. TCNOC (Twin Cities Norton Owners Assoc.) started it, now there can be 500+ weird bikes of all types in the parking lot in the summer, less in winter, but always a few, no matter what. From 5-11 pm. 607 W Lake St. 612-827-1726 Directions: 35 south to 35th St., west to Lyndale, north to Lake, right one block.

Whiskey Junction (**Minneapolis, MN**) Friday and Saturday evenings. Typical city 'bike' bar. Harley, Valkyeries, V-maxes, Gold Wings and a thin peppering of euro and sport bikes. 901 Cedar Ave S. Minneapolis, MN. Take I-94 to Cedar Ave. Exit. Go south. Located on Cedar Ave. 612-338-9550

Bob's Java Hut (**Minneapolis, MN**) Coffee bar + sandwiches. Lyndale Ave North of Lake St. Thrasher Vespa sidewalk surfboard haulers to immac wings (not!). Lots of older everyday rider bikes and seventies euro stuff. All the time, especially weekends. I-94 west of I-35 to Lyndale exit, south to 2651. 612-871-4485.

Betty's Bikes and Buns (**Minneapolis, MN**) Smooth espresso, juices, sandwiches, buns. Old gas station with tables out front in the driveway on a nice corner. Always some interesting bikes and urbanites alfresco. Evenings are best. 600 E. Hennepin, Mpls., MN 612-378-4988. Located in 'Nordeast', access from I35W by getting off on Washington exit, go west through downtown, take a right (north) on 3rd Ave., cross the river and bear right on Hennepin. Easy to spot.

Sir Benedicts Tavern on The Lake (**Duluth, MN**) Healthy sandwiches and many imported beers. Last Tuesday of the month, 6-10 pm. Euro, sport and odd stuff tire kicking and moto-geezer camaraderie, year round. 805 E. Superior St. I-35N to Lake ave, left one block to Superior St, right to 805. 218-728-1192

Fuel Cafe (**Milwaukee, WI**) Sandwiches & soft drinks. 7-12 weekdays, 9-12 Sat-Sun. Casual to punk. Kids. A nice variety of urban skoots come and go... but there's no special gathering time. 818 E Center St, Milwaukee, WI 53212. 414-374-3835. I-94 to I-43N to Locust exit right to Humboldt Ave to Center St, then right 2-3 blocks to 818 E (on the right side, center of block).

The Full Moon (**Lake Bluff, IL**) 24 hr restaurant, Sunday mornings, BMW's, Euros, Sport & whatnot. Better food than the Highland House. 1300 Skokie Hwy. 1/4 mi. S. on Hwy. 41 and Buckley Rd. (rt.137). 847-689-0733

Joe's on Weed Street (**Chicago, IL**) Restaurant. Sunday mornings Apr.-Oct. Touring, Cruisers, HD's, and all kinds of two wheeled arns. All you can eat buffet. 940 West Weed St. Exit 90-94 to Northome, East to Weed St., turn right to Joe's.

The Twisted Spoke (**Chicago, IL**) Biker themed restaurant with meat'n potatoes menu. No special gathering time. Mixed American and Euro bikes. North on Kennedy, Take Randolph Avenue, (3 lights) South on Kennedy. Take Ogden, go right one block. 501 N. Ogden Ave, Chicago. 312-666-1500

Ace Cafe (**Chicago, IL**) Brit Bike Rocker themed restaurant. Mmm. Brit food menu. Wednesday nights. Lots of Britbikes, scooteristes and Guzzis. 2025 W. Roscoe St. Chicago IL, 60618. 773-871-4300 From Kennedy, go north on Damon Ave. Go West on W. Roscoe St. <chefmoz.org>

Missouri Bar & Grill (**St. Louis MO**) Downtown bar with burgers. Evenings. First Tuesday of each month. Monthly EuroUnion MC meeting anchors a classic, sport and eurobiker crowd I-70 exit 10th St. to Cole St., right to Tucker St., left to 701 N. Tucker. 314-231-2234.

W.J. McBrides (**Overland Park, KS**) Restaurant/Bar. Evenings, 2nd Tuesday of the month. 12030 Blue Valley Parkway Eurobikes. 913-942-6904 Hwy 69 to Blue Valley Pkwy.

Coffee Bay (**Lenexa, KS**) Coffee house run by ex-pat South Africans. European/British bike-centered, but all are welcome. 9:00 a.m. on Saturday mornings @ intersection of Pflumm Road & 103rd Street in Lenexa, KS. (Lenexa is SW 'burb of Kansas City.) Homemade waffles. Shaded asphalt parking, outside seating. Simply wonderful.

The Other Place (**Overland Park, KS**) Bar and Restaurant. Wednesday nights. Mostly Harleys. 7324 West 80th Overland Park, KS 66204 913-652-9494 Santa Fe and 80th on the right hand side.

Cassoday (**Cassoday, KS**) Small Town - Tons of motorcycles. First Sunday of every month. Home of the Prairie Chicken(?) 45 miles NE of Wichita, KS, off of I-35.

Sunshine Café (**DeSoto, KS**) Restaurant/Coffee Shop. Sunday mornings. Euro and sportbikes. DeSoto is located between Kansas City and Topeka. Just off Highway 10. For more info, visit website <micoks.net>, or e-mail Van Stevenson at vanman01@email.msn.com.

Sports Page Inn (**St. Louis, IL**) South of Dupo. Evenings. First Tues. of each month. Monthly EuroUnion MC meeting anchors a classic, sport and eurobiker crowd. Second Tues. MCRA meets, a sport touring and sportbike crowd, promoting racing. At I-255 exit #9 (Dupo), go S on East Outer Road (2 miles), west side of road. 618-286-5628.

James Coney Island (**Houston, TX**) Hot dog chain fast food. Saturday nights late, esp. summer when the air's a little cooler. Sportbikes, poseurs and hot cars. 5745 Westheimer, Houston 713-785-9333. Directions: Go south on 610, go right (west) on Westheimer Rd., ride past the Galleria Shopping Center, cross Chimney Rock Rd., go a few blocks, you're there.

Specht's General Store (**San Antonio, TX**) Every Wed. night. Blanco Rd. North 7.5 miles from Loop 1604 to Specht's Rd. Turn right and it's a mile on the right. Mostly sport / sport tour with a lot of nostalgia and custom iron thrown in. Great food and laid back atmosphere. Draws large crowds in the summer.

Jo's (**Austin, TX**) Coffee shop with sandwiches and beer, too. First and third Wednesdays of the month, 7pm to about 9pm. All kinds of bikes from sport to kruzers 1300 S. Congress Ave. (Across from the Continental Club) Directions: Take I-35 south over the river bridge, go right (west) on E. Riverside Dr. Go left (south) on Congress Ave. So. past Academy Drive. A little ways down the road.

Marcus Dairy (**NYC**) Restaurant and Bar. Sugar Hollow Road, Fair Mall exit off I-84 at Danbury, CT. Mixed: cruisers, tourers, sport, etc... Sunday am's. Four special Sundays are "Superride" events which are huge crowds. (A hype-rally-scene with paid admission fundraiser.)

The Ear Inn (**NYC**) Restaurant and Bar. Sport, euro urban warriors, poseurs, pro racers. Every Tuesday night year 'round. 8-11 pm. 326 Spring Street (between Greenwich and Washington), Soho (Manhattan). Westside highway exit Clarkson. 212-226-9060.

The Bach Dor Cafe (**Hartford, CT**) Roadhouse tavern and cafe. Weekends. Lots of HD's, but well seasoned with a generous sprinkling of euro, sport and touring bikes. Intersection of Rt 6 and 98 in Chaplin, CT.

The Cloisters (**Philadelphia, PA**) Restaurant. Sport, euro and some cruisers. First Sunday of month, mornings. On US 322, Ephrata PA.

The Haag Hotel (**Philadelphia, PA**) Hotel & Cafe. Sportbikes'n tourers'n cruisers - backroaders to superslabbers. Mornings to mid-day on the second Sunday of the month. Good breakfast specials. South side of 3rd St. Sharlesville, PA. Exit 8 off I-78 between Harrisburg and Allentown. 610-488-6692

The Quaker Steak and Lube (**Sharon, PA**) Wednesday evenings. Larger 'event' type atmosphere. All kinds of bikes. HD's ubiquitous, euro and sport to the rear. 724-981-9464. Take I-80 west. Take the Sharon, PA exit, which is 4B. It's a four-lane highway. When it turns into two lanes, the restaurant is two blocks away.

Olney Ale House (**Olney, MD**) Bar and Restaurant. Sunday afternoons. Typical mix..Harleys, collectable bikes, hobby bikes, sport bikes. Good number of euro-sport bikes. Olney, MD. 301-774-6708. East of Gaithersburg and north of Washington, DC. From south: Take 270. Go N on 97 to 108. Head E about 2 mi. From north: Take 70 and turn S on 97 to 108. Head E about 2 mi.

The White Palace (**Purcellville, VA**) Bar and Restaurant. Every other Thursday evening. Euro bikes mostly. Some vintage. Some Sport types. 101 N. 21st St, Purcellville, VA. 540-338-2566. About 50 miles west of Washington DC. From west or south, take I-81. Take the Route 7 exit east. Ride for 25 minutes till you get to the Purcellville exit.

Paynes Biker Cafe (**Leesburg, VA**) Bar and bar food. Most evenings. Small place, small town. Harleys and a few euro bikes. 7 North King St. Take Route 7. It crosses 15th St. Cafe is on the corner of King St. (7th) and Market St. (15th).

Loch Raven Reservoir (**Baltimore, MD**) Parking lot overlook and turnout. Sportbikes. Saturday and Sunday am. From Baltimore, go north on #1 to Kingsville left (west) to Mt.Vista Road. Cross 147, go straight ahead. Take Williams Road to Gittings. Go straight ahead. Take Long Green Road, turn left (south) onto Manor Road. Turn right (west) onto Morgan Mill Road and pull into the parking lot.

Asylum Bar & Lounge (**Washington, DC**) owned by the former proprietors of the now-defunct Crow Bar, the Asylum features permanent, camera-equipped bike parking in front. 2471 18th St. NW, Washington DC 20009. 202-319-9353. Calvert St. So. to 18th St. NW.

Whites Ferry (**Washington, D.C.**) Roadhouse restaurant and convenience store. Weekends. Sport, Euro, Hogs, general adult type motors. On Whites Ferry Rd, 6 mi S of Rt 28 and 4 mi N of Leesburg.

Michael's Bar & Grill (**Chapel Hill, NC**) Good ol 'merican food and drinks. All kinds of good ol' motor bikers. Sunday am locals, and assorted curves-r-us friends. Cole Park Plaza, Right off Hwy 15-501, South of Chapel Hill. 919-942-6904

Arby's (**Hickory, NC**) Fast food place. Thursday nights. All bikes from sport to trike wings things. US Hwy 321 NW in Hickory. 828-324-9429

Euclid Ave Yacht Club (**Atlanta, GA**) Bar/full restaurant. Harleys and cruisers. Little Five Points area. 1136 Euclid Ave. NE, Atlanta, GA 30307. Take 75 east or west to 20. Go east on 20. Take Moreland Ave. NE to the north (left). Go left on Euclid Ave. N. 404-688-2582.

Vortex (**Atlanta, GA**) Thursday evenings. Sportbikes. Little Five Points area. 438 Moreland Ave. NE, Atlanta GA 30307. Take 75 east or west to 20. Go east on 20. Take Moreland Ave. NE to the north (left). 404-688-1828

$3 Cafe (**Atlanta, GA**) Cafe/Restaurant. Sunday all day. All kinds of bikes. Rich people. Buckhead area. 3002 Peachtree Rd. NW, Atlanta GA 30305. Take 85 north. Go north on 400. Go left (west) on Peachtree Rd. Cafe is at intersection of Peachtree Rd. and Roswell Rd. 404-266-8667.

Happy Days (**Pompano Beach, FL**) Fifties fast food diner. Exclusively Rokon Trailbreakers and MZ Silver Stars, yeah that's it...Rokons and MZ's...uh huh. Last Saturday of the month. 7:30 pm til 9 pm, shine or shine only. 351 SW 12th Ave. Pompano Beach, FL. 954-784-0055

Top Dog Cafe (**Stuart, FL**) Upscale bar & cafe... Upscale usually means Hardly-Ableson's. Thursdays 6-9 pm. Exit I-95 East to Stuart. At US100 left into Publics Shopping Center, Top Dog is on the left side. 860 S Federal Hwy, Stuart FL 34994. 561-287-9110.

Denny's (**Orlando-Apopka, FL**) Coffee Shop Restaurant Sunday mornings by 8. Brit, Italian, German and other sporty bikes. NW from Orlando on I-441 to Apopka - right beside the highway.

Everglades Holiday Park (**Ft. Lauderdale, FL**) Snack Bar. Sunday Mornings. Cruisers, Sportbikes, Euro Bikes. Corner of Rt 27 and Griffin Rd. 800-226-2244

The Flying Swan (**Vancouver, BC, Canada**) Chinese coffee shop and cafe. Sport and euro bikers. Motorcycle Mondays, Hot Chick Tuesdays, etc... 1724 West 4th Ave, Vancouver, BC Hwy 99/99A to Seymour St, south about three blocks to 4th ave, right 1/2 block on 4th to 1724. <www.flyingswancoffeehouse.com> 604-737-4945.

Some Good Roads

Alabama
- AL 117/TN-56

Alaska
- Hwys 1, 2 and 3
- AK 8 from Cantwell to Paxton (gravel)

Arizona
- Hwy 666/191 from Clifton to Springerville
- US 89A from Flagstaff to Prescott
- AZ 83 from Mtn View to Sonoita

Arkansas
- AR 88/OK 1
- AR 7 from Hot Springs to Harrison
- AR 341

California
- Hwy 89 through Lassen National Park
- Hwy 1 from SF to San Louis Obispo
- E on 76 to Rincon Springs, R on S6 to S7, to CA76, L to CA79, R to S2, L to S22
- CA 9 from Saratoga to Santa Cruz
- CA 25 from Gilroy to CA 198, left to Coalinga
- Skags Spring Rd from Stewarts Point to Geyserville
- CA 49 from Slattley to Grass Valley
- CA 58, west from 33

Colorado
- US 34 through Estes Park
- Grand Lake US 34 to Granby to US 40 to Empire
- CO 141 to Naturita, to CO 145 to Telluride (or L on 62)
- CO 149 from US 50 near Gunnison to South Fork
- US 50 from Pueblo to Grand Junction

Connecticut
- 169 to Woodstock W from Hartford on 4, at Harwin 118 to Litchfield, then US 202 to New Preston, then N on 45 to US 7, then back to Hartford on US 44
- 39N from Danbury to 37 N to Sherman, then 39 to Gaylordsville, then N on 7 to Cornwall Bridge, then L on 4 to Sharon, then 41 to Lakeville. R on on 44 to Canaan to Winsted, 8 to 20 North

Delaware
- US 9 Laurel to Lewes
- DE 9 Delaware City to Dover

Florida
- Hwy 27
- US 1 from Florida City to Key West
- from Orlando NW on 441 to 437 S to 438 W to 50 W to 455NW to 19 N to Tavares

Georgia
- Hwys 60/180
- Dahlonega N on US 19 to US 76 E to Hiawasse

Hawaii
- Hwy 200

Idaho
- Hwy 15 and 77
- ID 21 from Boise to ID 75 to US 26
- US 12 from Kooskia to Lolo, MT (Lewis & Clark Hwy)

Illinois
- US 30 West
- Freeport on US 20 to IL 84, S to Fulton

Indiana
- Hwy 135 through Brown Country to Kentucky border
- Bloomington E on IN 46 to Columbus, S on IN 7 to Madison to 56 to 156

Iowa
- Hwy 2, Des Moines
- Great River Road (hwy 52) from Bellevue to Lansing
- L 34 N from Weston to Logan

Kansas
- Hwy 99
- KS 177 S from Manhattan to Council Grove to US 77 to Arkansas City

Kentucky
- Hwy 11 through Boone National Forest
- Lexington 168 South to Harrodsburg, then US 127 and 150 SE to Mt Vernon, then N on I75 to KY 169

Louisiana
- US I-90 from New Orleans to Houma

Maine
- Hwy 27 Kingfield to Canadian border
- N from Bar Harbor on 3 to Ellsworth, E on US 1 to Whiting, NE on 189 to Lubec (Easternmost town in USA) to Canada 774.
- from Belfast N on 7 to Sangerville, W on 16 to 6/15m then N to Jackman, then S on 201 to Walkerville
- ME 9 from Bangor to US 1

Maryland
- Hwy 12/ US 113 Salisbury to Pocomoke through Pocomoke Forest
- 144 from Sideling Hill Cut to Keysers Ridge, then 219 to Deep Creek Lake
- 213 from Fair Hill to Centerville

Massachusetts
- Hwy 2
- 62 from Barre to Burlington
- 202 from Orange to Belchertown

Michigan
- MI 22 from Manistee to Mackinaw City
- MI 119 from Harbor Springs to Cross Village

Minnesota
- US 61 Duluth to Grand Marais
- MN Hwy 1 Illgen City to Ely

Mississippi
- Hwy 1
- Natchez Trace Parkway

Missouri
- Hwy 136 across northern Missouri
- MO 5 from Mansfield to Ava, W on MO 76 to MO 125 to MO 76
- MO 100 W from Hermann to US 50 W to 179 North to I-70 E to Mo 94 to Hermann(?)
- MO 79 from Hannibal to St Peters
- US 19 from Steelville to Alton
- MO 32 from MO 21 to Success
- MO 14 from Dogwood to US 63 near West Plains

Montana
- Hwy 83 through Glacier National Park
- 43 W from Divide to Wisdom, then 278 S to Dillon
- US I-90 from Deer Lodge to MT/ID border
- US 200 trans-MT from ND border to ID border
- US 212 (Bear Tooth Hwy) Silver Gate to Red Lodge
- US 191 from Bozeman Hot Springs to West Yellowstone
- US 2 Browning to West Glacier
- MT 37 Libby to Eureka

Nebraska
- Hwy 2 Grand Island to Alliance
- US 20 from Sioux City to Harrison

Nevada
- Hwy 278
- US 93 from Ely to Vegas

New Hampshire
- Hwy 112

New Jersey
- Rt 542 through Basto
- Old Mine Road NE from Kittatinny Ridge to Montague then County 521 and NJ 23 to US 206

New Mexico
- Rt 532
- US 84 from Santa Fe to NM503 to NM76 to Taos to NM 75 to MN 518 to NM 68
- Silver City W on 180 to 78, then W to Guthrie (Arizona)
- Rt 4 from San Ildefonso (near Santa Fe) to San Ysidro
- Rt 152 from Hillsboro to San Leandro

New York
- US 9
- NY 30 to NY 3 to NY 86 back to NY 30
- NY 54a from Hammondsport to Branchport
- NY 301 from McKeel Corners to Carmel

North Carolina
- Hwy 16
- US 17 from Albemarle to New Bern
- S from Sylvia on US 441 to 107, then S to 1001, then to Higdonville, then W on 64/28 then R on 23/441 to 116, then R to 107
- NC 226A Little Switzerland to Blue Ridge Pkwy

North Dakota
- Rt 1084 along Missouri River

Ohio
- US 52
- US 50 to Chillicothe to OH 159 NE to Lancaster to US 33 to US 22 to Zanesville then N on OH 60 and 16 to Coshocton
- OH 350 W from Cuba to I-71
- OH 555, S of Columbus, Wayne N.F.

Oklahoma
- AR 88/OK 1

Oregon
- US 101 along coast, Astoria to Brookings
- OR 242 W from Sisters to 126, then L to Springfield
- Nestucca River Road, Carlton to Beaver

Pennsylvania
- Rt 44 Jersey Shore to NY state line
- US 30 west from Philly then PA 897 N to PA 340
- PA 31, West Newton to Napier
- PA 219 from Somerset to Salisbury, then West on 669 to Listonburg
- PA 641 from Newville to Shade Gap, then 522 South to Waterfordsburg

Rhode Island
- Rt 102
- US 1 and 1A to Watch Hill
- 138 to Newport

South Carolina
- Cherokee Foothills Scenic Hwy

South Dakota
Rt 87 through Custer State Park

Tennessee
- US 64 east to west
- TN 73 from Townsend to Smokey Mtn Park, Laurel Creek Rd to Little River Rd E to Newfoundland Gap Rd US 441 to Cherokee
- Tellico Plains E on TN 143 to North Carolina 143 to Robinsville

Texas
- Rt 16 San Antonio to Kerrville via Bandera
- from Bandera N on 173 to Center Point, then E on 27 to County 473, then R on Upper River Rd to 473
- US 75 Richland to Willis
- County 1431 from Cedar Park to Bluffton
- County 696 from Baxter TX 2, then left to Bryan

Utah
- Rt 14 Cedar City to US 89
- UT 12 from Torey to Bryce Canyon National Park

Vermont
- Rt 100 north to south
- Talcville W on VT 73 to 53, then N to 7 to East Middlebury
- 9 from Wilmington to Bennington
- VT 17 from Waitsfield to S. Starksboro

Virginia
- Blue Ridge Parkway
- VA 56 from Vesuvius to Roseland, then 655 to Colleen

Washington
- Rt 165 up the backside of Ranier
- US 101 from Olympia to Olympia
- WA 20 from Rockport to Twisp
- Forest Service Rd 33 from Carson to FS 51, to FS 90, to FS 25 to Randle

West Virginia
- US 19
- Petersburg W on VA 55 to VA 66 East to I 64 to US 220 back to Petersburg
- VA 39 from Summerville to Buena Vista (Virginia)

Wisconsin
- Rt 35 Prairie du Chien to Prescott along Mississippi River
- US 95 from Blair to Fountain City (also local 'alphabet' roads)
- Rt 60 from Sauk City to Prairie du Chien

Wyoming
- US 287
- US 89 N from Jackson to US 20 to WY 120 to WY 296 to US 212
- US alt 14 from Dayton to Lovell

All American Roads

These roads are special. They have been designated All American Roads, the highest federal highway designation. They were chosen based on scenic, cultural, historic, archeological, recreational and natural characteristics. All American Roads are considered destinations unto themselves that best represent the United States. For additional information <http:www//byways.org>

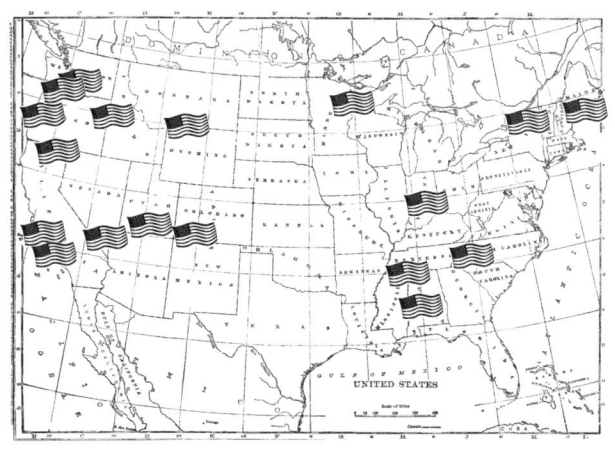

The Seward Highway
AK 1 to AK 9
Anchorage, AK to Seward, AK
Natchez Trace Parkway
NCP MI, AL, TN
Natchez, MS to Nashville, TN
Selma to Montgomery March
AL 80
Selma, AL to Montogomery, AL

Route 1, Big Sur Coast
US Hwy 1
Carmel, CA to San Luis Obispo, CA
San Juan Skyway
CO 160 to Cortez, CO 145 to Sawpit, CO
62 to Ridgeway, CO 550 to Durango
Durango, CO to Durango, CO
Trail Ridge/Beaver Meadow Road
CO 36 to CO 34
Estes Park, CO to Grand Lake, CO
Acadia Byway
ME 3 circles Acadia National Park
Trenton, ME to Acadia NP, ME
North Shore Scenic Drive
MN 61
Two Harbors, MN to Grand Portage, MN
Beartooth Scenic Byway
MT 212
Red Lodge, MT to Yellowstone NP
Blue Ridge Parkway
Blue Ridge Parkway National Park
Great Smoky Mt. NP to Shenendoah NP
Las Vegas Strip
Las Vegas Blvd.
Russel Road to Sahara Ave.
Hells Canyon Scenic Byway
OR 86- to FR 39 FR 39- to Enterprise OR 82- to LaGrande
Baker City, OR to LaGrande, OR
Chinook Scenic Byway
WA 410
Enumclaw, OR to Naches, WA
Historic Columbia River Highway
US 84/OR 30
Portland, OR to The Dalles, OR

Volcanic Legacy Scenic Byway
62 to Crater L. NP Junction, OR
OR 138 to Diamond Lake Junction
Klamath Falls, OR to Diamond Lake OR
Mather Memorial Parkway
WA 410 to WA 12
Enumclaw, OR to Natches, WA
A Journey Through Time Scenic Byway
Hwy 12
Red Canyon, UT to Torrey, UT
Lakes to Locks Passage: The Great Northeast Journey
Various roads including NY 98, NY 22, and US 4.
Waterford, NY to Rouses Point, NY
The Historic National Road
Many signed roads roughly paralleling I-40, which in turn replaced
the 'National Road' originally surveyed in 1822.
Baltimore, MD to St.Louis, MO

Accommodations and Reservations

Call ahead at a mid-day stop to learn what is available within the afternoon's riding range. Many chains will provide driving directions in addition to reservations. Rooms usually have many prices based on the immediate demand. Always ask about discounts from the quoted seasonal 'rack rates'.

Best Western International, 800-528-1234.
Budget Host Inns, 800-283-4678.
Choice Hotels, 800-221-2222.
   Clarion Hotels
   Comfort Inns
   Econo Lodges
   Friendship Inns
   Quality Inns
   Roadway Inns
   Sleep Inns
Courtyard By Marriott, 800-321-2211.
Days Inns Of America, 800-325-2525.
Doubletree Hotels, 800-222-8733.
Embassy Suites, 800-362-2779.
Fairfield Inns, 800-228-2800.
Hampton Inns, 800-426-7866.
Hilton Hotels, 800-445-8667.
Holiday Inn, 800-465-4329.
Homewood Suites, 800-225-5466.
Hospitality International, 800-251-1962.
   Downtowner Motor Inns
   Master Host Inns
   Passport Inns
   Red Carpet Inns
   Scottish Inns
Howard Johnson, 800-446-4656.
Hyatt Hotels, 800-233-1234.

ITT Sheraton Hotels, 800-325-3535.
La Quinta Inns, 800-531-5900.
Marriott Hotels, 800-228-9290.
Motel 6, 505-891-6161.
Omni Hotels, 800-843-6664.
Park Inns International, 800-437-7275.
Preferred Hotels, 800-323-7500.
Radisson Hotels, 800-333-3333.
Ramada Inn, 800-272-6232.
Red Roof Inns, 800-843-7663.
Residence Inns By Marriott, 800-331-3131.
Stouffer Hotels, 800-468-3571.
Super 8 Motels, 800-800-8000.
Travelodge, 800-578-7878.
Westin Hotels And Resorts, 800-228-3000.
Wyndham Hotels and Resorts, 800-996-3426.

Campground Associations

Most of these associations will answer the phone from 8pm - 5pm and can provide telephone contact numbers and driving directions to local campgrounds. They also can provide a list of campgrounds in their state.

Alaska Campground Owners Association, c/o McKinley KOA Kampground, P.O. Box 340, Healy AK 99743. 907-683-2379.

Arizona Travel Parks Association, 1130 East Missouri - Suite 530, Phoenix AZ 85014-2717. 602-230-1126.

California Travel Parks Association, P.O. Box 5648, Auburn CA 95604. 916-885-1624.

Colorado Association of Campgrounds Cabins & Lodges, 5101 Pennsylvania Avenue, Boulder CO 80303. 303-499-9343.

Connecticut Campground Owners Association, 14 Rumford St., West Hartford CT 06107. 203-521-4704.

Delaware Campground Owners Association, c/o Seasons Camping Resort, P.O. Box 156, Rehoboth Beach DE 19971-0156. 302-227-2564.

Florida Association of RV Parks & Campgrounds, 1340 Vickers Drive, Tallahassee FL 32303-3041. 904-526-7151.

Idaho RV Campgrounds Association, 11101 Fairview Ave., Boise ID 83704. 208-345-5755.

Illinois Campground Association, P.O. Box 7471, Springfield IL 62791. 217-546-2794.

Indiana Recreational Vehicle Council, 3210 Rand Road, Indianapolis IN 46241. 317-247-6258.

Iowa Association of Campground Owners, c/o Timberline Best Holiday Trav-L-Park, 3165 Ashworth Rd., Waukee IA 50263. 515-987-1714.

Kansas Campground Association, c/o Malm's Smoky Valley Plazza, Box 175, Lindsborg KS 67456. 913-227-2932.

Kentucky Campground Owners, Pioneer Playhouse, Rt. 2, Box 12, Danville KY 40422. 606-236-2747.

Louisiana Campground Owners Association, P.O. Box 4003, Baton Rouge LA 70821. 504-346-1857.

Maine Campground Owners Association, 655 Main St., Lewiston ME 04240. 207-782-5874.

Maryland Association of Campgrounds, 9800 Cherry Hill Road, College Park MD 20740-1210. 301-937-7116.

Massachusetts Association of Campground Owners, RR1 - Box 3040, Kennebunk ME 04043-0998. 207-985-4864.

Michigan Association of Private Campground Owners, P.O. Box 68, Williamsburg MI 49690-0068. 616-267-5089.

Minnesota Association of Campground Operators, 1000 E. 146th Street - Suite 121, Burnsville MN 55337. 612-432-2228.

Mississippi Campground Owners Association, c/o Biloxi Beach Campground, 1816 Beach Blvd., Biloxi MS 39531. 601-432-2755.

Missouri Association of RV Parks & Campgrounds, 3020 South National - Suite 149, Springfield MO 65804. 314-564-2551.

Montana Campground Owners Association, c/o El-Mar KOA, 3695 Tina Avenue, Missoula MT 59801. 406-549-0881.

Nebraska Association of Private Campgrounds, c/o Fort McPherson Campground, RR. Box 142, Maxwell NE 69151. 308-582-4320.

New Hampshire Campground Owners Association, P.O. Box 141, Twin Mountain NH 03595. 603-846-5511.

New Jersey Campground Owners Association, 29 Cook's Beach Road, Cape May Court House NJ 08210. 609-465-8444.

New York Campground Owners, P.O. Box 497, Dansville NY 14437. 716-335-2710.

North Carolina Campground Owners Association, 1002 Vandora Springs Road - Suite 101, Garner NC 27529. 919-779-5709.

Ohio Campground Owners Association, 3386 Snoufer Road - Suite B, Columbus OH 43235. 614-764-0279.

Oklahoma Association of RV Parks & Campgrounds, c/o MarVal Trout Campground, Rt. 1 - Box 314M, Gore OK 74435. 918-489-2295.

Oregon Lodging Association, 12724 SE Stark St., Portland OR 97233. 503-255 5135.

Pennsylvania Campground Owners Association, P.O. Box 5, New Tripoli PA 18066. 610-767-5026.

Rhode Island Campground Owners Association, Box 141, Hope Valley RI 02832.

South Carolina Campground Owners Association, c/o Ocean Lakes Campground, 6001 South Kings Highway, Myrtle Beach SC 29575. 803-238-5636.

South Dakota Campground Owners Association, P.O. Box 620, Black Hawk SD 57718 0620. 605-787-6836.

Tennessee Association of Campground Owners, c/o Little River Village Campground, 8533 State Hwy. 73, Townsend TN 37882. 615-448-2241.

Texas Association of Campground Owners, P.O. Box 14055, Austin TX 78761. 512-459-8226.

Utah Campground Owners Association, c/o Temple View RV Resort, 975 South Main, St. George UT 84770. 801-673-8400.

Vermont Association of Private Campground Owners, c/o Homestead Campground, RD 3 - Box 3454, Milton VT 05488. 802-524-2356.

Virginia Campground Association, 2101 Libbie Avenue, Richmond VA 23230-2621. 804-288-3065.

Washington Association of RV Parks & Campgrounds, c/o Minerva Beach Campground, 23215 76th West, Edmonds, WA 98026. 206-283-5210.

West Virginia Recreational Vehicle Association, 205 First Avenue, Nitro WV 25143. 304-727-7431.

Wisconsin Association of Campground Owners, c/o Bass Lake Campground, N 1497 Southern Road, Lyndon Station WI 53944. 715-839-9226.

Wyoming Campground Association, c/o Foothills Motel & Campground, P.O. Box 174, Dayton WY 82836. 307-655-2547.

Notes On Gear

These appendices are supplemental to the 'Gear-everybody will do this a little differently' section earlier in this book. They are specific notations about gear that was used on a specific trip by one individual. All riders will come to varying conclusions regarding what is necessary and what works for them through hard-won experience. These notes are included as an example for further thought. Each letter below (A-K) refers to the equipment and items listed on pages 9 and 10.

A. Modified Honda XR650L--The motard conversion means it is easy to handle and fun on curvy paved roads, even carrying about 35 lbs of travel and camping gear. The larger gas tank is desirable everywhere and critical in sparsely populated areas, which include most of the midwest, west and mountain states. A 200 mile range should be the minimum.

B. Front Fender Bag--Most of the time the bike cover is carried in the front fender bag so it can be deployed to cover the bike for security with or without removing or opening any other packs. Sometimes the electric vest is carried here. The vests simple on/off switch is lighter, smaller and more field-repairable than a thermostat. I switch the heat on or off in combination with slightly opening or closing jacket vent zippers to provide a comfortable microclimate.

C. Number Plate Bag--All the little stuff. Lip balm carried here goes into a jacket pocket when it turns hot, sunny and dry. The faceshield rag is for my glasses (and also the helmet shield when there's no paper towels on the gas pump island). Ditto the squeegee-edged Clearview spray bottle of soapy water. The refillable butane cigarette lighter is for starting campfires, lighting the camp stove, and for melting fraying webbing and nylon fabrics. The Suunto Vector instructions are in case I need to use this wrist computer for more than just the time and temperature. The spare Suunto battery is the size of a quarter and is carried 'just in case'. This device needs a new battery at unpredictable but-always-inconvenient times about every two years. The sidestand plate is for the rarely encountered soft surface where no stones, sticks or flattened cans are available. The aspirin and ibuprofen is for the occasional hangover, headache or muscle ache. If a headache seems to be starting, taking an aspirin before riding prevents it from becoming worse. Ibuprofen can have the same helpful effect for a post-crash or over-exertion related muscle strain. The low tech five bladed 'boy scout style' Swiss Army Knife is light, small and does just about all the jobs a heavier and more complex multi-tool will do, but in a simpler package. Even without a locking blade it's terrific for opening packaged foods, trimming split cuticles, spreading peanut butter, cutting webbing and a zillion other things. I like a clear helmet faceshield and sunglasses combination. Reading glasses or a spare pair of prescription glasses are carried because my eyes need them. The spare ear plugs are for when I lose the ones that are forgotten in a jacket pocket. Thin Thermax glove liners fit under my elkskin ropers (just barely), but are seldom used. If it's too cool for the electric grips alone, I switch to a mid-weight insulated glove with a gauntlet. The Thermax glove liners add insulation and work even better with these. The dry Evap-O-Danna goes around my neck in cold conditions and is saturated with water on hot days. The sun hat is for protecting my bald head and keeping the sun out of my eyes. It is deployed practically the instant my helmet comes off. Sometimes I carry the sun hat in my jacket's chest pocket. The best sun hats are made from lighter and more packable fabrics. A bill or brim is essential. Dorky looking hats are worth double points when traveling with wives or girlfriends. The glove raincovers get used only if I'm sure it will rain for more than a short period. The trick is to commit to putting them on before the leather gloves get soaked, which is harder than it sounds. It's usually tempting to ride just a little farther because the conditions might improve. If it's a rainy day, I'll transfer the left raincover to my jacket's left pocket and the right one to the right side. There, they are easy to pull on quickly. On straight wide roads with little or no traffic I'll sometimes do this with the throttle locked, wobbling along unsteadily for about a mile. Most of the time I'll pull into a driveway or onto a wide shoulder and then put them on while the bike idles. The Petzl Zipka is my main all-around flashlight. I like it's long life LED bulbs, compact size and built-in (self retracting) headband. Before this model was introduced I used a LED Tronics 'Mag' type AA flashlight which was attached to an Aerostich tri-mount flashlight headband. This was a good setup, but the Petzl does all the same jobs in a smaller, lighter package.

D. Handlebars and Map Case--The folding mirror is an enduro tool designed to minimize crash damage and be used in dense woods riding, but it also comes in handy for overnight covering. When folded down, the mirror also hides the GPS perfectly. The Sunnto Vector wrist top computer gives the time of day, elevation and ambient temperature. It can also be worn as a spare wristwatch if needed. The GPS III is a multi-function time/speed/distance navigation tool that can also function as a precise voltmeter. It is hardwired so it can be on continuously while riding. The radar detector/radio bracket is a small acrylic platform that holds a scan/seek AM FM radio. It positions the radio so all of the controls can be easily operated with the left hand. The radio is shrink wrapped for water resistance. 3M makes a great window insulating film that uses the heat of a blow drier to shrink. It's perfect for making any exposed electrical device more water and dust resistant. On this size motorcycle having a radar detector is not critical. Time spent at higher speeds is minimized because of limited horsepower and little wind protection. The Cycoactive map case holds current maps where they can be read and used at a glance. This quick-detach envelope also holds a pen, a grease pencil that's clipped on the left side and ready for instant writing on the window, and any other papers that might be needed at a moments notice (like toll road, ferryboat or parking ramp tickets). The electric grip switch is positioned near the left side so it can be frequently toggled off and on without needing to take one's hand off the throttle. A friction type flip-lever cruise control provides wrist relief and allows the right hand to be used briefly for a variety of other purposes.

E. Aerostich Waterproof Side Zip Bag #3--A Bibler I-Tent for solo trips or an Ahwahnee for two. West of the Mississippi a 'footprint' ground cloth protects the tent floor from rocky campsites. Performance sandals are my only off-the-bike footwear from June through September. They are versatile, comfortable and pack small. Worn with sox they are warm, and they are useful for lakes, swimming holes, and public or campground showers. A good pair can be walked in for miles or worn into fancy hotels and restaurants. They're all the off-bike footwear I need. The microfiber pants and shirt go on and off during the day for a variety of reasons and at a moments notice. I've zipped the legs off the pants for an impromptu swim in a roadside lake. They are good for both sun protection and warmth off the bike, and add insulation under riding gear on cool days. They'll wash clean in a sink with a bar of soap and are fully dry in minutes. The microfiber pants are my second pair of pants, after blue jeans. They're perfect for more formal situations or when the jeans are being washed. Microfiber pants are cooler-wearing than jeans in sweltering conditions. On cold days I can use them with the blue jeans and Darien riding pants for three combined layers of insulation. Microfiber clothing is ultra-packable, too. The cell phone charger carried here can be connected to the bike while inside the packed duffel bag to allow recharges while on the move. Carried mostly for emergencies, the phone normally rides in the upper pocket of my riding jacket where it can be quickly reached. The water bottle is carried full and ready for roadside use. In hot and dry conditions it is sometimes carried on the outside of the pack, beneath only a strap or bungee.

F. Aerostich Waterproof Side Zip Bag #2--After experimenting with a variety of sleeping pad thicknesses and lengths, the 3/4 Thermarest is the smallest and lightest one I'm comfortable sleeping on night after night. Combined with my riding pants and jacket, it makes a nice full length bed. The tent light is a row of LED's set in a clear acrylic dog bone. The lamps are connected to the motorcycle battery by a twenty foot power wire. It's a nice feeling of security to know there is a wire running directly from your bike right into your tent. The funny dog bone shape both stores the wire and makes it easy to hang the light up in a tent. In a fit of fussiness, I filed all of its sharp edges into smooth radiuses. The sleeping bag is a goose down summer weight mummy. It's stuffed directly into the side zip bag without a separate stuff sack. This makes it faster to pack and unpack every day, and the waterproof zip bag keeps it dry and secure in all conditions. The bear spray is for people or bears, but in years of traveling has yet to be needed. It's replaced every few years with a fresh canister.

G. Aerostich Waterproof Side Zip Bag #3--I carry a microfiber towel because they are highly absorbent, pack small and dry fast. Mine's large enough for fully drying off after washing or bathing. The swimsuit has pockets and can double as shorts. The food bag is a large Aerostich envelope bag that always contains some chopsticks, a titanium spoon, a bottle of Tabasco sauce, a small salt and pepper shaker…and whatever fresh, dry and canned consumables I've purchased at stores along the way. The thin 100wt fleece sweater is great for general evening wear or insulation over the electric vest on cold days. The daily trip journal and its zippered cordura cover serve as a roadside office. Besides the journal notebook it holds: Spare pens, receipts, contact lists, some hidden money, assorted travel papers and whatever else I need to keep administrative track of. I try to add some notes in the journal every day or two.

H. Ortlieb Small Drybag Duffel--Two pair of sox are plenty. Every couple of days I wash out one pair in a sink. It takes only minutes. The Smartwool t shirt is for dress-up evenings and cooler days and nights. The other two t shirts are for sleeping and everyday wear. One is black and the other is a lighter color, but both always carry some stupid artwork or credo. The Tank Bag Briefcase bag is where I keep a couple of paperback books, some traveling money, receipts transferred from the daily journals zippered binder, a complete library of applicable trip maps, some small amounts of postage stamps/postcards/envelopes, a small address book and a few related incidental items like paper clips. The camp stove lives inside a nylon bag within the cook kit, along with a small microfiber kitchen towel, a pan scrubber and a couple of folding utensils. A refillable aluminum fuel bottle packs separately. I try to keep this container vertical, even though it's never spilled or leaked a drop of fuel. The bottle is refilled from the motorcycle's gas tank by disconnecting the fuel line from the carburetor and opening the petcock. The cook kit consists of a pot and lid-pan. A drink mug is packed nearby. The folding water bag is unrolled and filled at campsite taps or is used wherever a larger volume of water needs to be temporarily carried for later use. When full the bag can be carried directly on top of the other packed duffels. The bathroom kit contains a nail clipper, tweezers, small first aid kit, some over-the-counter meds, vitamins, a folding comb/hairbrush combo, a small tube of toothpaste, and a toothbrush which sheathes into a sewn nylon sleeve that protects the bristles yet allows them to dry while packed. There's also a small container of stick deodorant, another with some dandruff shampoo, and a bottle of all-purpose Dr. Bronners soap. This liquid soap is good for general bathing, dishwashing and laundering, and is biodegradable enough to be safe for direct use in streams and lakes. A drinking-cup-shaped cordura fabric sleeve holds about half of these personal items and nests inside a small titanium cup which itself is carried within the bathroom kit. Also carried inside the kit is a tiny 1" liquid filled compass which is useful for determining where the sun will rise and for navigating during post-ride reconnaissance walks from a motel room or campsite. An Avocet Vertech wristwatch with a soft hook&loop wrist strap completes the kit. This tool works as an alarm clock and also tells the ambient temperature in my tent. It also shows elevation and the barometric trend. It can be a wristwatch, too. For anyone counting, this is the third wristwatch: One on my wrist, one on the bike's handlebar and this one. The camera and film are for recording stuff, though when traveling alone about all the use it gets is for immortalizing campsite locations for later reference. When with others it gets used more. Did I mention the titanium flask of scotch whiskey? I started carrying a flask years ago when it seemed like good insurance against a lying-in-a-roadside-ditch-injured-and-in-pain scenario. Now it's carried for campfire nitecaps.

I. Rear Fender Toolbox--The Honda's stock tools are upgraded with a better pliers and screwdriver. I like the 7" Knipex adjustable jaw plier which spreads large enough to clamp around steering stem and axle-sized nuts. A small Vise Grip® locking pliers is added, along with a Leatherman multi-tool, various kinds of replacement wire, a couple of chain master links, a small roll of silicone electrical tape and duct tape, and some spare light bulbs (tail light, signals, instruments). A bicycle tire pump, inner tube repair kit, some co2 tire fillers and titanium tire irons provide tire fixing capabilities. An adjustable prop stand works in combination with the motorcycle side stand to hold a wheel off the ground. It makes daily chain lubing much easier. Old bicycle and motorcycle inner tubes that have been cut into rubber bands of a variety of widths are so useful that I always carry a few. The Cycoactive Tow Downs work as either a tow strap or tie downs. They're handy if the bike must be transported on a helpful strangers truck or trailer. The C-H Bungee buddy is a good way to carry any kind of bulky object and can be deployed on top of the rest of the pack or used when the bike is unloaded. Two pair of spare earplugs are kept here just in case the other two pair become lost. The ear plugs of last resort. The rolled up spare inner tube fits either of the 17" motard wheels if the patch kit fails. For chain lube I carry a bottle of 90 wt gear lube or chain saw bar oil. Aerosol chain lubes are much neater but cost more and they're empty in just a few days. My thick polyethylene lube bottle came from a drug store and originally held some kind of cosmetic or hygiene product. It has a nice applicator tip and packs inside a leak resistant Aerostich envelope bag. A colorfully monogrammed shop towel completes the rear fender tool ensemble. The custom embroidery on this towel is an exact replica of the bike's wiring diagram. Not.

J. Darien Jacket Right Sleeve Pocket--The LED Fingerlight flashlight attaches to my left gloved index finger. After dark I can point it at the liquid crystal ambient temp thermometer or the road map to read the route or directions. It clicks on and off by pressing it's lens against the handlebar or rear view mirror stem. I've also whipped it out more than once at a campsite or parking area to find something accidentally dropped in the grass. The Vee Wipes carried are two sizes. One's primarily a spare, but having both sizes is nice when the temps and glove thicknesses vary. Sometimes the spare earplugs are spare earplug speakers. In the inside chest pocket: The cell phone is a Motorola M60 flip phone, a model chosen more for its small carrying size than the function and feature set. In the other inside pocket: The cotton bandanna (or folded paper towels) have a zillion uses from wiping noses to cleaning face shields and headlights. In remote areas I'll sometimes carry a half roll of T.P. flattened inside a ziplock bag in an outside pocket.

K. Darien Pants--Wallet; mine's brown leather from a department store and contains two or three credit cards, lists of telephone numbers, money, two quarters for pay phones, family photos, a few business cards, a drivers license and some insurance information. It goes in the left front pants pocket because sitting on it all day while riding is not comfortable.

Measurement Conversion

If You Know	Multiply by	To Find
LENGTH		
inches	2.540	centimeters
feet	30.480	centimeters
yards	0.914	meters
miles	1.609	kilometers
millimeters	0.039	inches
centimeters	0.393	inches
meters	3.280	feet
meters	1.093	yards
kilometers	0.621	miles
WEIGHT		
ounces	28.350	grams
pounds	0.453	kilograms
grams	0.035	ounces
kilograms	2.204	pounds
VOLUME		
fluid ounce	29.573	milliliters
pints	0.473	liters
quarts	0.946	liters
gallons (U.S.)	3.785	liters
milliliters	0.033	fluid ounces
cubic inches	0.01639	liters
cubic inches	0.0043	gallons

TEMPERATURE

°C = (°F -32) x .555   °F = 180 (°K - 273.15) - 32
°F = (°C x 1.8) +32   °K = °C + 273.15
°C = °K - 273.15   °K = 0.555 (°F + 273.15) - 32

INCHES	DECIMALS of FOOT	MILLIMETERS
1/4	.020	6.3500
3/8	.0313	9.5250
1/2	.0417	12.700
5/8	.0521	15.875
3/4	.0625	19.050
7/8	.0729	22.225
1"	.0833	25.400
2"	.1667	50.800
3"	.2500	76.200
4"	.3333	101.60
5"	.4167	127.00
6"	.5000	152.40
7"	.5833	177.80
8"	.6667	203.20
9"	.7500	228.60
10"	.8333	254.00
11"	.9167	279.40
1 Foot	1.0000	304.80

Mileage Calculator

GALLONS USED

Miles Travelled	1	1.5	2	2.5	3	3.5	4	4.5	5	5.5	6	6.5	7	7.5	8	8.5	9	9.5	10
20	20	13	10	8	7	6	5	4.5	4	3.6	3.3	3	2.8	2.7	2.5	2.4	2.2	2.1	2
40	40	26.6	20	16	13.3	11.4	10	9	8	7	6.6	6	5.7	5.3	5	4.7	4.4	4.2	4
60	60	40	30	24	20	17	15	13.3	12	11	10	9	8.5	8	7.5	7	6.6	6.3	6
80	80	53.3	40	32	27	23	20	17.7	16	14.5	13.3	12.3	11	10.6	10	9	8.8	8.4	8
100	100	66	50	40	33.3	28.5	25	22.2	20	18	16	15.3	14	13.3	12.5	12	11	10.5	10
120	120	80	60	48	40	34.2	30	26.6	24	21.8	20	18.5	17	16	15	14	13	12.6	12
140	140	93.3	70	56	46.6	40	35	31	28	25.5	23.3	21.5	20	18.6	17.5	16.5	15.5	15	14
160	160	116	80	64	53.3	46	40	36	32	29	27	24.6	23	21	20	19	18	17	16
180	180	120	90	72	60	51.4	45	40	36	33	30	28	26	24	22.5	21	20	19	18
200	200	133	100	80	67	57	50	44	40	36	33	30	28	27	25	24	22	21	20
220	220	147	110	88	73	63	55	49	44	40	37	34	31	29	27.5	26	24	23	22
240	240	160	120	96	80	68	60	53	48	44	40	37	34	32	30	28	27	25	24
260	260	173	130	104	87	74	65	58	52.2	47	43	40	37	34	32.5	30.5	29	27	26
280	280	187	140	112	93	80	70	62	56	51	47	43	40	37	35	33	31	29	28
300	300	200	150	120	100	86	75	67	60	54.5	50	46	43	40	37.5	35	33	31.5	30
320	320	213	160	128	107	91	80	71	64	58	53	49	46	43	40	38	35.5	34	32
340	340	227	170	136	113	97	85	75.5	68	62	57	52	48.5	45	42.5	40	38	36	34
360	360	240	180	144	120	103	90	80	72	65	60	55	51	48	45	42	40	38	36
380	380	253	190	152	127	109	95	84	76	69	63	58	54	51	47.5	45	42	40	38
400	400	267	200	160	133	114	100	89	80	73	67	61.5	57	53	50	47	44	42	40
420	420	280	210	168	140	120	105	93	84	76	70	65	60	56	52.5	49	47	44	42
440	440	293	220	176	147	126	110	98	88	80	73	68	63	59	55	52	49	46	44
460	460	307	230	184	153	131	115	102	92	84	77	71	66	61	57.5	54	51	48	46
480	480	320	240	192	160	137	120	107	96	87	80	74	68.5	64	60	56	53	50.5	48
500	500	333	250	200	167	143	125	111	100	91	83	77	71	67	62.5	59	55.5	53	50

Notes

Notes

Notes

Notes

Notes